The Law In Shambles

The Law In Shambles

Thomas Geoghegan

PRICKLY PARADIGM PRESS
CHICAGO

Prickly Paradigm Press, LLC
5629 South University Avenue
Chicago, Il 60637

www.prickly-paradigm.com

ISBN: 0-9728196-9-X
LCCN: 2005921571

Printed in the United States of America on acid-free
paper.

Prologue
A Warning at the Red Mass

At the Red Mass, the Bishop from Rockford told us why our rule of law is in shambles. A "Red Mass" is held for judges and lawyers before the Supreme Court begins a new October term. By luck, I once hit upon the true Red Mass, the kind to which the US Attorney General, the Solicitor and a few Justices like Scalia come. They pick up their robes to kneel down for a blessing.

Even a judge who is not Catholic might like to mingle with a bishop. For judges and bishops have certain sartorial things in common. Both of them wear a lot of red and black. Both have to put on dresses.

When men rise to a star-chamber type of power, it seems they have to walk around in skirts. Being a lawyer, I just wear suits. But that autumn morning in D.C., at St. Matthew's, I was glad not to be in red or in black.

But at the Red Mass, the homilist lauded us all because we love the rule of law. Indeed the Church, which is the Roman Empire in embryo, also loves the rule of law. For centuries the bishops, like St. Augustine, in Hippo, functioned as judges. Bishops like St. Augustine actually held court. They heard civil cases. The Church is still around because when the dark ages descended from time to time, it was willing in a pinch to stand in for the state.

So that morning, as I knelt there with the Justices for the blessing, I had a sense of solidarity with all these alpha males in velvet. Cardinals. Judges. The Red. And the Black. I thought: how lucky are those who are able to go to court.

After that experience I wanted to go to more Red Masses. Turns out that in Chicago, where I live, we have a Red Mass too. We have a Cardinal, indeed a very smart one. We have some judges too. But there's no Justice Scalia. No Justice Thomas. Some of the judges at our Red Mass are in Domestic Relations and Traffic Court.

But a judge in Traffic Court deserves a Red Mass too.

And that's how I came to be in the pews, in November 2004, when the homilist turned out to be the bishop from Rockford, Illinois. Rockford! What a place to be a bishop. As my brother who goes up there a lot says: "It's got all the disadvantages of living in a big city, with all the disadvantages of living in a small town." What a come down after the Vatican. The bulletin said this bishop had lived in Rome, where he studied the canon law. He had practiced canon law and now he was in Rockford. So after years of reading Aquinas in Latin and testing the carpaccio in Tuscany, he was raising money in Rockford and eating pizza from the carry out.

But when he started his homily, I forgot about Rockford.

The bishop was really smart. And in an erudite way, he was uneasy about the rule of law. He began with a little joke, in Latin, involving the patron saint of lawyers, Saint Ivo. He said: *Advocatus, et non latro, et mirando populo.*

I knew what it meant: "A lawyer and not a thief, and therefore a wonder to the people." My partner Leon Despres had once translated it for me.

And having quoted this dark saying, the bishop began to talk even more darkly about the law today. A chief characteristic of the law, he said, is that the people accept it as legitimate. That is the essence of the law. "And if people do not accept a law as legitimate, it brings all law into disrepute. And if all law is in disrepute," he concluded, "that in turn leads to anarchy."

To what law was the bishop referring?

I asked the man sitting next to me at the Red Mass breakfast later that morning if he knew. He didn't know. "And did you get what he was saying to us in Latin?"

"No," he said.

Funny, too, because he was a Jesuit. So I translated.

"Oh."

"Well, that was the least of it," I said. "Why did he keep saying that people have to accept the law as legitimate?"

"I wondered about that," said my new friend.

"And if they don't accept a law as legitimate, it calls every law into disrepute?"

Neither of us knew.

"Well," I said, "I'm sure he didn't mean it, but someone could say: 'Well, Bishop, here's an argument from Church tradition, or Aquinas, why we shouldn't have a law banning abortion. If you do, and if people don't accept it as legitimate, it's going to call every other law into disrepute.'"

"I don't think he meant that," said the Jesuit, quietly.

Well, no. I'm sure he didn't. But that's what opponents of the Church might well point out: If the Church got its ban, most people in this country would not regard it as legitimate. And would it not call every other law into disrepute?

But let's not get into that. It's the never ending argument. Besides, I was interested in the Bishop's hint that people in America might no longer accept the rule of law as legitimate.

For here was a man of the Vatican. And I would say to people on the left: if it does not touch on faith or morals, the Vatican can be dispassionate. It can be a pretty cool observer. Because in Rome they know the world, and the world is a good judge. And if the world judges that there is something shaky now about the rule of law in America, maybe we should pay some heed.

And do not others think the same?

A few years ago I met a woman from Russia. She was in the United States on a short visit.

I said: "So how's America?"

Oh, it's good. It's fine. It's great. But then she lit her cigarette and dropped her voice: "Something is wrong here. What is it?"

More and more, people in other countries have begun to notice, too. We torture detainees. We break our treaties. We start pre-emptive wars. And whether it's a bishop or a Russian lady, most people around the world may still believe: America! It's fine. It's good. It's great.

But something is wrong here. What is it?

Well, as a lawyer, I'd say: We have changed the law in a big way—I mean the law you and I experience in our daily lives. And it all seemed to happen without anyone's consent. And so I've entitled my little homily: *The Law in Shambles*.

It's a little longer than the Bishop's; I hope it doesn't clear the pews.

Chapter One
Do We Have Too Much Democracy?

Fareed Zakaria, the youngish *Newsweek* columnist, has a nifty op-ed argument, which he has blown up into a book: *The Future of Freedom: Illiberal Democracy at Home and Abroad*. Zakaria's point is this: In the Third World and in America, there is too much democracy, and too little rule of law. Zakaria then tries to connect "illiberal democracy" in countries like Iran with illiberal democracy in America. Roll back democracy. And let's have more judges and lawyers. Let's have the elite make up the rules.

Now, it seems hard to believe that America of all countries suffers from too much democracy. In 2000 we "elected" a President who lost the popular vote. We have a Senate where forty Senators representing less than nine percent of the population can block any bill. We have a House in which under a tenth of the seats are seriously contested. There is so little democracy that in a typical presidential election only half of the country even bothers to vote. It's about a third or less in "off-years," like 2002, when the issue is merely the control of the House and of the Senate. Often just a third will decide who will be governor of a major state.

That's too much democracy?

Apparently in both Iran and in America Zakaria wants more elite rule, insulated from the mob. Here are his examples: the Federal Reserve Bank; the Pentagon; the US Supreme Court. They work great! Take the Court. The Justices deliberate. They act reasonably. They can save us from the caprice of Congress. They can save us from the sense that the world is arbitrary, irrational.

This is an old Whig argument. It is the argument on behalf of rule by powdered wigs. For centuries, they have been saying: Before there can be democracy, there needs to be the rule of law. And that means: the *Magna Carta*; the *Domesday Book*; Blackstone. The work of centuries—let's not rush into Democracy! Because Democracy is arbitrary and irrational. Look at Congress. Too much democracy can undermine the rule of law.

Now, this would seem to be an argument from the right. Except in America, on the right, conservatives like Robert Bork despise and hate judges. In Bork's recent book, *Coercing Virtue: The*

Worldwide Rule of Judges, he rages against lawyers and judges. He seems to hate them all. Indeed, he seems to rage at the idea of the rule of law itself.

Anyway, is Zakaria right? For this really is his claim: that in Iran and America, we have too much democracy. We need more rule of law. OK. Well, I don't know much about Iran, but it seems to me he has it backwards. Seems that Iran has too much rule of law, and not enough democracy.

But let's take America. Do we have too much democracy? Maybe if there were fewer of us voting, we'd have more rule of law. I doubt it, but let's assume there would be more stability, etc., etc. Why is that good? Because we'd know what our rights were. And in this respect Zakaria may be on to something. People in the United States might be happier if they knew what to expect, if they knew what their rights were. Maybe they would be happier. Maybe they would stop experiencing the world as arbitrary and unpredictable. I would be happier, certainly—as a lawyer. I would stop experiencing the world as arbitrary and unpredictable.

Yes, if that's all he wants, I think Zakaria is on to something. And the Bishop of Rockford is on to it too. In Rockford, and all over, people experience the world as more arbitrary, unpredictable. Or at least my clients seem to feel it—more and more.

But is Zakaria right, that we have too much democracy?

Well I admire Zakaria for writing his book, and maybe one day, in another pamphlet, I can give the man his due. But no, I don't think he's right. He is terribly wrong. It's the lack of democracy in our country, today, which undermines the rule of law. As more people drop out of civic life, it has had a negative, corroding effect on the law. The law is less stable, less predictable. And as it becomes less stable and less predictable, people tune out.

But first of all, why would anyone say we have too much democracy? In the 1996 presidential election, for the first time, over half of eligible voters didn't even vote! That's a cosmic kind of thing, isn't it? In *The History of European Civilization* (1827), Francois Guizot described that HISTORY as one in which more and more people take part in decisions. He found it hard to imagine the opposite—the process going backward, or fewer and fewer taking part in decisions.

True, one can claim this reverse process is happening in other countries. But how did it happen in such a big way in America?

Let me talk about Three Big Facts. Around each of the three facts I have tried, pretentiously, to write a separate book. The first Big Fact is the collapse of American unions. How did this happen? As I tried to explain (in book #1): through the gradual loss of the right to join a union, freely and fairly, without being fired. Without that right, the labor movement in America collapsed. In 1958, its unions covered thirty-four percent of the private sector. Maybe more, say some historians. And in the North and Midwest, where the real economy was, the percentage was much, much higher.

In 2005, labor is down to seven or eight percent of the private sector. Who could have guessed it back in the golden age of 1958?

In a sense, the flowering of the New Deal came years after FDR. By the right to bargain through unions, we came more than half way to European-type welfare. It was a private-sector kind of socialism. Company by company, in a rocky, uneven way, more Americans got pensions, health care, supplemental unemployment benefits. By the 1960s, in the steel and auto industry, workers were even getting European-type vacations, every four years, like a sabbatical. If it was not universal—if it was not "Europe" for all of us—it was "Europe" for more and more of us.

As in Europe, people became not just "political" citizens with the right to vote, but "social" citizens with the right to certain benefits. If I was a citizen, it meant I had "rights." These rights, though "legal," were not constitutional. They were contractual. But it did not seem to matter: The rights to pension, to health, and to vacations would keep on spreading as if they were constitutional. But they weren't constitutional. And they didn't keep on spreading. These rights—not the negative ones (i.e., of liberty), but the positive ones (i.e., of property)—and the pursuit of happiness began to disappear.

Why? Because labor collapsed. I wish there were another reason, because I'm a labor lawyer. And for a labor lawyer to blame it all on One Fact seems pretty self absorbed. OK, I am sorry. And indeed I can say labor collapsed for more than One Reason. There were several. The law created a real problem: The Wagner Act, for example, has no sanctions when employers fire labor organizers. But there was also the "nationalization" of the economy. That is to say, the

South and West opened up. As employers moved there, they discovered how illusory the right to organize really was. They found out they could break the labor laws, and nothing would happen. There were no real sanctions, no penalties. And because of Taft Hartley and state laws that outlawed secondary strikes—and boycotts, and mass picketing—labor could no longer hit back.

So we entered an era of mass civil disobedience: not from civil rights marchers, but from companies. They simply picked out pro-union workers and fired them, blatantly, in violation of the Wagner Act, because the Wagner Act had no teeth. It seemed we in labor could do nothing—or that what we could do just cost too much. As each organizing drive became a legal battle, labor ran out of money. It also ran out of nerve. And I must admit, as incomes began to drop, the higher wage unions did not care to, or really know how to, organize the lower wage workers.

Today we're too weak to help them. Too weak, I fear, even to help our own. In the 1950s and 1960s we were strong enough to raise not only our own but everybody else's wages. Whatever the labor people got, everyone else got: pensions, health care, living wages. That kind of labor movement is gone.

In no other developed country, at no other time in history, has there been such an explosion of inequality. GDP soars, productivity soars. Incomes go down. But we have lost more than just income. Often there is:

- No pension
- No health insurance

(or it's the kind with staggering $5,000 deductibles)
• No vacation (literally)
• No sick pay (in fact, you can't even call in sick)

That was Fact One.

I've also tried to write around another Big Fact. Big Fact Number Two is the drop in the voting rate. Or, put another way, the withdrawal from civic life. It's not just that we are no longer "social citizens" with social or economic rights. For we have lost pensions, health care, vacations. We make less and less an hour. (And I blame all that on the collapse of labor.) So now, more and more of us are resigning as "political" citizens. More of us feel we no longer have a stake in our country; we don't owe it a vote. In the 2000 election, which came after my book on Big Fact Number Two, alas, fewer than 47 percent of eligible male Americans cast a vote. (Women, God bless them, voted at 53 percent.) And the young hit a new low.

But then of course we had the uptick in 2004. So do I take it all back? In the wake of the election, editorial after editorial read: "Voter apathy is dead!" "Mass turnout!" "Five hour waits!" Oh come on. It did go up—to 57 percent. But in part we got this higher percentage by playing around, subtracting more people from the list of so called eligibles, including ex-felons and "illegal aliens." That is, the percent of turnout is increasing because we put more and more people in prison. And we don't want our maids and valets to vote either, even though they may have worked for us for years. In Florida there are over 600,000 ex-felons barred from voting, but they account for one-and-a-half of Florida's electoral votes. OK, they aren't "eligible." But even so, if we apply the same constant measures in recent elections, the turnout for Bush vs. Kerry went up by only three percent. Three! That's after massive registration and beating on doors and MoveOn.org and America Come Together and the awakening of the entire religious right, and the expenditure of four billion dollars, total, on all races in 2004. Four billion to get a blip of three percent! And this in an election that was supposed to be as epochal as that of 1860. All told, 2004 was a drop in the turnout from 1992, and is perfectly consistent with the evident downward trend.

The Third Big Fact is prison. Since I got out of law school in 1975, the number of people in prison has increased by a factor of seven.

Recently, a young person asked me: "What was it like in the 1960s?" I could have said something about Janis Joplin and drugs and women's liberation. But instead I said, "What was it like? Oh, well, nobody in the country was being executed." I might have added: Even in Texas. Can you imagine? In the 1960s hardly anyone was in prison either. I guess it was a strange answer. Later, I wondered: What prompted me to say that, of all things? I must have been trying to say: In the 1960s, we had this freedom, which we no longer know we once had.

I know a man, a reporter, who has to cover prisons as part of his beat. When he talks to a prisoner the first time, he likes to ask: Does anyone ever come to see you? The answer is: No.

"It's always the answer," he said to me.

While none of us may think of prisoners, some of us may feel that we too are breaking some laws. If you happen to read Isaiah or the Gospels, for example, it's pretty clear we're all supposed to be down there visiting the people in prison. But the scriptural problem aside, I wonder if our prison culture undermines the Constitution. Put it this way: instead of celebrating equality under the law, more of us are developing the moral character of guards.

By the way, how did we get millions of our fellow citizens in prisons? Answer: the labor law collapsed. (Sorry, I really do have one answer for everything.)

We could also say the hourly wage did it. Richard Freeman, a labor economist at Harvard, has made much of the shocking 30 percent drop in hourly wage for young men—a drop which happened just as the crime rate shot up in the 1970s. So these young men, especially minorities, looked for a "living wage" by going into crime. Being a labor lawyer, and blinkered anyway by only one or two big ideas, I tend to look at things the way that a labor economist like Freeman does. It's all related to the hourly wage. The rate of crime, as the Victorian economists used to say, is tied directly to the price of bread.

So while each book I wrote has its own little Big Fact, there is really but One Big Fact which loops in and out of the others: The Unfairness of It All. Most of us get less and less, even as the country as a whole gets more and more.

As this inequality gets worse, I have seen big changes in the legal system. We may still be equal before the law. For now. Maybe. It's arguable. But even if it's true for now, how much longer can it last? As inequality gets worse, our super-rich, even if under-taxed, will pay the bulk of the taxes. And why pay for a rule of law that applies to all of us equally?

I can't even use a term like "us" to describe the country now. In an op-ed I read in late 2004, the economist Robert Shiller of Yale estimated that the bottom 40 percent of American families, by income, used to account for 18 percent of all national income. Now it's under 14 percent. Soon, he said, it may be under ten! At ten, it's hard to imagine all of "us" really under a single rule of law.

To make matters worse, inequality is destroying the moral character we need for any stable rule of law. The rich feel less and less responsibility for the rest of us. But it's the middle class that worries me. There is good reason to think the middle class is becoming more corrupt.

Corrupt? Yes. Consider this single fact: It took ten years—almost all of the 1990s—for the median family income to get to the same level that it was, in real terms, in 1989. But in 1999, when we got to the same income level we had in 1989, the "median" family had to work six more weeks a year.

To keep from falling, the 1999 middle class had to work six more weeks a year for free. Not a few more hours. Six more weeks! By the way, maybe it's worth pausing to say: No wonder our GDP keeps shooting up, if the middle class is being forced to work for free.

But all this unpaid extra labor tends to under-mine the rule of law.

Why? The economist John Maynard Keynes put it best: "Nothing corrupts a society more than to disconnect effort and reward." That's what did in the old Soviet Union: no matter how hard one worked, one could not get ahead of someone who did not work at all. And that is what is happening in America, too. Of course, in a certain way our country would seem the very opposite of the Soviet Union: here, if people don't work, they're going to end up being homeless. Then again, if they do go to work they may end up being homeless too.

That's the point. Like the USSR, we are slowly breaking the connection between effort and reward. And that's a dangerous thing to do, in terms of the rule of law. It's dangerous to push the middle class into questioning the fairness of the rules.

The danger is that people in the middle class will begin to see the world as arbitrary and unfair—unpredictable, a matter of luck, a chance of catastrophe around the corner. It does not matter if they work the extra hours. Over 40 percent of American families have less than $5,000 in savings. One bill, out of the blue, can blow everything away.

So quietly, and to themselves, people at the median or below have to wonder, as the country becomes fabulously wealthy: Why play by the rules?

I may even understate the case. The disconnect between effort and reward is much greater than it seems from the figures that I gave on income. Many people really did not get back to the same 1989 level of income in 1999. Think of pensions. Fewer people had them. Think of health insurance. Fewer people had it. And perhaps our moral character can survive one decade of that kind of thing, but it's kept on going.

Why is this so dangerous for the rule of law? It's simple, I think. If we do not expect the world to be reasonable and fair, then sooner or later we do not demand or expect it from the law. We get used to the arbitrary and unfair. Sometimes, we take a certain glee in it—at least when arbitrary things happen to others. But in our own lives we experience it as alien. We did not consent to it. We did not vote. And we take no responsibility for what the rule of law becomes. And worse, the more we drop out, the more arbitrary and unpredictable the rule of law does indeed become. The unions, political parties and other institutions like the liberal churches helped us shape a certain legal system. When they began to weaken, the law itself began to change. It became, as I hope to show, less rational and predictable. It is not just that people now perceive the law as less rational and predictable. It really is.

Still, the less rational and predictable it becomes the more we go along. Because more and more people experience the rule of law in the same way they experience the world.

But in what way is the rule of law becoming less rational and predictable? Well let me list these big changes, to which in any conscious or deliberate way most of us did not agree.

Chapter Two

From Contract to Tort:
Or, How We Experience the Rule of Law at Work

There is a thesis by the British historian, H.S. Maine, that the movement from tradition to modernity is one from "status" to "contract." Without being quite as grandiose, I say the biggest change I have seen, though it is not put this way in the legal literature, is that, with the collapse of the New Deal, we have moved from "contract" to "tort."

For most working Americans, this may be the biggest change in the way the law now impacts their lives. In the 1950s and 1960s, up to 35 percent of workers, especially men, were covered by collective bargaining agreements. As a matter of "contract," each worker could not be fired, except for just cause. If he were fired, his union would file a grievance and argue that "just cause" did not exist under the contract. If it was not resolved at the grievance step, an arbitrator came in and decided the case in a cheap, informal procedure, often without a lawyer. The remedies? Reinstatement. Back pay. The idea was that under a contract, a "relationship" would continue, in some way. If only between the employer and the union.

"Contract" also permeated the non-union world. For the cultural norm, back in business then, was: what the hourly worker got, the middle manager got. If it was not a contract as such, it was at least a contract-based norm of fairness.

Now, from what I can see day to day in my own practice, this world of "contract" is gone. Few workers—under nine percent in the private sector—operate under any kind of labor contract. The rest work under a rule of law known as "employment at will." That means you can be fired for any reason. Or no reason. Or a bad reason: like the color of your tie. At any time. With no warning. No severance pay. Nothing. Once in Berlin for some European law students, I taught a seminar on US labor law. At the start of our first class, I told them about "employment at will," kind of as an aside. I found, to my dismay, that in each subsequent class I'd have to explain, all over, about "employment at will." For European kids, it was too hard to take in. Get fired for any reason? At all? The arbitrariness, the unfairness of it, was shocking. It was new to them.

While it may sound like "old" law, in a way it's new for us. Yes, we talk of "employment at will" as common law, as if it went back to King Arthur and his Court. But in America, we are firing people as we never have before. After the New Deal, Americans worked under a "contract," or a threat of one, through union organizing. For most of our history, we have lived in an agrarian nation. We farmed, or learned trades, in small towns. The old America needed labor. That's why we used to bid up wages.

In short, until unions collapsed, America did not know "employment at will" in anything like its current, universal, and highly arbitrary form. Far from being an old tradition, "employment at will," is, for us, like a Brave New World. It means a turnover unlike that in any other developed country. It is a regime that many Americans experience as infuriating, without being able to express any fury.

And that's why they invented "tort."

I hardly need to tell an American what is a "tort." But in case you are from Greenland, I better define it. In the law, it is a wrongful act—not for breach of contract or breach of trust, but an injury, for which (usually) you ask for some relief in damages.

A tort is money for pain. It's a howl from the roof of a building. It's a claim for a broken arm, or maybe the invasion of privacy.

The point is, when we strip so many people of a contract, some of them are going to fire back in tort.

So now in the workplace, while there is no right to sue in contract, there is often one in tort.

Since the collapse of unions, Americans have flooded the federal courts with "civil rights" type claims, analogous to claims in tort. As labor (or contract) law waned, civil rights (or tort) law waxed. Indeed, this waxing and waning come right out of Congress. For over thirty years, unions have tried to pass labor law reform, to modify the Wagner Act, to let Americans join unions. Freely, fairly—without being fired. While coming close, the unions have lost over and over in the US Senate, by small margins, usually as a result of a filibuster. But perhaps as a consolation prize, Congress will frequently add another "new" civil right: for race, age, sex, handicap.

Sorry, no contract. But here's another civil right claim, i.e., another right to sue in tort. There are so many such rights now it is tricky even for us veteran lawyers to know in a given case which tort best applies. You come to me, and say, "I'm fired."

Here is just a short list of the laws I have to think about:

- The Civil Rights Act of 1964, as amended in 1991
- The Civil Rights Act of 1871
- The Age Discrimination in Employment Act of 1976
- Employee Retirement and Income Security Act of 1974
- The Occupational Health and Safety Act
- The Family and Medical Leave Act of 1994
- The Warn Act of 1991

Oh, and are there more? You bet there are. Just in the 1990s, in the federal courts alone, the number of civil rights cases more than tripled. And there are even more laws at the state level.

So this is the world not of labor law, but employment law. Not of contract but of tort law. And now in our federal courts, at least on the civil side, it is the biggest type of law. Each year in federal court in Chicago we see thousands of these cases. Forty percent of all the filings, a magistrate judge told me. But this new tort law is meaner and more complex and costlier than contract.

First, it is not so much about conduct as state of mind. The issue is no longer whether the employer fired the plaintiff for "just cause," whatever that might now mean in a world of "employment at will." What the plaintiff must do is show that the employer acted to harm him. The point of the case is not to limn one's "objective" or "external" act but the "subjective" or "interior" intent, in a sense to peer into the human heart.

In other words, the issue is "motive." But as to motive, it is unclear even now, at least at the trial level, what a judge on a given day may require us to prove. Right now, on appeal, the firm I work at has a case involving race. And the issue for the appellate court is: does race have to be "the" factor? Or only "a" factor? Surely, it is the latter.

OK. But if only "a" factor, then what kind of "a" factor? Does it have to be a controlling factor? Or only, as some say, a catalytic factor, as the judge declared in our case? Or does it only have to be a substantial factor? We say: not catalytic but only substantial. Do you agree? Then there is another big issue: whether, even if race is a factor, the employer can still win by showing he would have done the same darned thing anyway.

Confused? So are the lawyers. After 40 years, and 40,000 case opinions, and repeated attempts by the Supreme Court to clarify, we are on appeal, and the case law is, I can assure you, still unsettled.

How is that possible? Because no one formula is both narrow enough and wide enough to work for every case. The jury comes back with a question. And then we're on appeal.

Second, compared to the old contract law, the new tort or civil rights law is expensive. Contract (arbitration) was cheap. Easy. But now the fired employee has to come up with big money: five, ten thousand dollars—not to pay my legal fees but just for costs (the court reporter, depositions, photocopying).

Of course, by a court award I have to obtain my fees from the other side. Soon, I have a cash claim bigger than my client's! I have just looked at my "bill" for a single Title VII case, so far, to date, with no trial: it's nearly $180,000!

The old system? The whole proceeding would cost under $10,000. For both sides.

Third, for one reason or another, the cases never go to trial—either because the federal courts drop them through one or other legal "trap door," or the parties, exhausted, finally settle. That's true of most civil litigation. Of 100,000 civil cases in federal court, perhaps fewer than two percent will go to trial. Recently, the *New York Times* did a front page story about the fact that lawyers in America no longer try cases. The puzzle in the story was: why settle on the eve of trial when the parties have already "sunk the costs" in the litigation? By the time of a trial the big expenses are over. The trial itself, which may be two or three days, is not that much more expensive. Oddly it may be that because the parties have paid out or "sunk" so much in cost, after all the deadly, destructive discovery, they are more risk averse than ever. Besides, no one is sure what instructions may go to a jury.

Fourth, the new tort law is much more scorched-earth style than the old contract law. For one thing, in federal court, unlike arbitration, I can use the rules of discovery. I can force you to tell me everything—what is in your secret heart. Not to mention what's in your tax returns.

It's hard to exaggerate how big a change this is: everyone in the case has to strip themselves in a sense, take off their clothes, far more now than was the case when I started out in law school. Look at what Paula Jones' lawyers did to Bill Clinton—and he was a sitting President. What makes the new "American-style" tort law so bitter, so arbitrary, is discovery, with each side on a rampage to swing at the other's head.

Over what? Intent, motive. A "bad" state of mind. That gives a legal rationale to harass and destroy, in a litigation that is disconnected from whether the employee was treated fairly.

Obviously, it is terrible for the employer, and he or she is often right to complain. After all, the employer did not engage in a "hate" crime or, probably, fire because of race. Or it was a mix, not one bad motive. But it was the employer that got rid of the older, cheaper system. For the more expensive the system, the broader the discovery right, the bigger the employer's advantage. It is the management lawyers who first showed us, the plaintiff lawyers, how to torture people in a deposition!

And with the new tort, unlike the old contract arbitration, there is no need to hold back on slash-and-burn. In the old arbitration, the remedy was to re-instate. To put the employee back. If both employer and employee had to live together again, like a married couple, it made no sense to slash-and-burn. But in the tort system, nobody is going back. Not now. Never happens. For one thing, the litigation will take years. And go back to be fired again? So even if the parties could hold themselves back, there is no longer any reason to.

In post-union America, this is the legal system we now have. It forces us to cast legal issues in the most subjectively explosive way, i.e., "racism," "sexism," to get around the fact that we no longer can deal objectively with "just cause." Do I regret I am part of it? Yes. Are my clients often full of hatred? Yes. It is also frightening how much power I have as a lawyer in any civil case. The other day at lunch a younger lawyer complained to me: "Oh, the other side, it never gives you what you ask for. I'm so disillu-sioned with being a lawyer, etc." How often do I hear this? I said to him: "Do you realize how much power you do have? You have more power than a subcom-mittee of the US Senate! When a committee holds hearings, it has but a few months to subpoena, and the White House resists, etc. Then it's over, with little coughed up in the end. While in a private case, like Paula Jones, it is possible that a lawyer can subpoena, then go back, then subpoena, then go back, and do it at leisure, for years, much in the same way as a Special Prosecutor. In a certain way you, as a 26-year-old lawyer, may have more power than the entire US Congress to bring down a sitting President! How can you complain?"

My point is that this tort-type legal system, which replaces contract, is a system that feeds on unpredictability and rage. A white-hot, subjective tort-based system with the threat of "discovery" replaces a cooler, more rational, contract-based one which was modest, and cheap, and kept us from peering, destructively, into one another's hearts.

Chapter Three
From the Law of Trusts to the Collection Courts:
How the Charities Came to Prey on Beneficiaries

To me, in my life, an even bigger change has been the flight from trust law, or the law of charitable institutions. Today, the "charities" which are supposed to take care of us try to hunt us down. They sue the people they are supposed to help. Hospitals sue the poor. Colleges sue kids, straight into bankruptcy, and beyond. Oh, how I miss the law of trusts! It was this old charitable law which appealed to my tender side. I was going to work in pension law, in health law, which had its foundation in the law of trust, the law of charity. Or so

I figured when I left law school. But this law which had lasted from the Tudors to Gerald Ford blew up when the unions collapsed.

Let's go back to 1975-76, when I just got out of school. In 1975-76, most working Americans had become part of big charitable trusts, i.e., pension and health funds. Most of these funds are now gone. This is a big shock to people: there is no longer a trustee or fiduciary to take care of them. And here too, this big change in the law of trusts comes out of labor's collapse.

Thanks to labor, we had come to have a nation of charitable trusts, i.e., of pension funds subject to the law of trusts. Often these were big multi-employer plans. They had "defined" benefits, i.e., you got that big pension even if the Dow collapsed. Now if we have anything, we just have 401(k)s. That's a voluntary savings account. The boss does not save, as in the old system. You and I save.

Sure. We Americans are famous for saving, right? Ha ha. Result: no one has a pension. I exaggerate, but not by much—at least for people who make under $100,000 a year. (Even, to my shock, in the case of some friends, people who make over that! Yes, I know it's America, but can't they save something?)

When we were in these legal charities, our trustees collected money from our bosses, and held it for us in trust. We the People couldn't get it, even to spend it to send our kids to college. We were the "beneficiaries." We had trustees or fiduciaries. They saved us from ourselves. It is a weird thing to say, but they had a legal duty to love us. Under the Employee Retirement Income Security Act, or ERISA, the trustees had, and still have, duties in the law, of "prudence," of "diligence," of "care," of "loyalty." No, I'm not joking: That's what is in the law. They have a duty to take care of us, in the same way they might take care of themselves. And so thanks to ERISA, a certain kind of love is law. They passed ERISA as I was about to come out of law school. Oh, the older people told me, this will change our lives. It was a big deal: maybe not as big as Social Security but to some of us as big, or bigger, than Medicare.

ERISA would spread the law of trusts to every-one. At least to everyone in those big plans that had "defined" benefits and were typical of the time. How many were in such plans? Over half the work force. So half of us now came under the care of guardians. Or trustees. We could work till old age and know someone would take care of us.

Now, years later, it turns out no one will be taking care of us.

When labor collapsed, employers stopped offer-ing pensions—at least of the "defined benefit" kind (a fixed sum, like $2,500 a month). It's the kind for which the employer, not the employee, has to "save." But with this wonderful ERISA, how could the employer just stop giving a pension? Well, the law never said the employer had to give a pension. Once the pressure of dealing with a union vanished, employers either: (1) stopped offering any pension; or (2) pushed people into 40l(k)s, or "defined contribution" arrangements.

And as people found out, when they landed in the 401(k)s—baby, they were on their own. The employer might, or might not, match.

In a country where savings is less-than-zero, the concept of a 401(k) plan, i.e., that most of us, house-poor and broke, would voluntarily fund our own pensions, is fantastical. And soon, the "defined benefit" pension will be gone. Except for a few cops and teachers. And for the rest of us? Theresa Ghilarducci, a labor economist at Notre Dame, estimated that, in 2000, at the height of the economic boom, the average 401(k) individual plan had no more than $24,000—the average. She included the top fifth of wage earners, who stash away millions. Indeed the 401(k) plan is an engine of inequality. People at the top build up their own by taking it from the people below. I mean this literally. I was recently visited by a 401(k) consultant, who asked me, as he asks other employers, if I might want to "restructure" our firm's 401(k), to "appropriately reward" the "high-end earners." In other words, we should take it from the secretaries and give it to ourselves. He had closed the door of my office.

Why not? Steal it from her. No one would know.

Well, I won't say what I did. But whatever it was, no one would find out. The trustee, the old-fashioned trustee of the big ERISA plans, is gone. No one is there to stop people like me from bleeding my secretary's tiny account, without her ever knowing. So little people beware. But it's more than just the risk that I may be "restructuring." The investment companies and banks that run these little savings accounts often cheat people, one by one, in nickel and dime ways. Because there is no real trustee around, the companies pile on "fees" and "charges" for handling the accounts, so any gain that poor secretary makes in the market is wiped out by a higher, usually hidden fee. It's terrible. Quite eloquently, a friend of mine, John Wasik, a financial columnist, has written about the way people are ripped off. Why don't we lawyers bring suits? Because the cheating is too small, microscopic, and hard for us to detect.

In this new world of little accounts, there are no fiduciaries—though they may say so on the bank cards or on our accounts. In truth, there is no one to save for us. Or to stop the restructuring or the hidden fees.

So what happens? Without grasping what is going on, many people get less of a pension year by year. Of course if they turned it all over to Enron or Worldcom, they ended up with little or nothing at all. Because no 401(k) is insured, the way the old defined benefit plans are insured by the government.

In some 401(k)s, the employer "matches" what you or I save. But why bother now to match? With no unions, the only reason the employer may set up a 401(k) is for tax reasons. And as the Bush Administration keeps slashing taxes, there is less cause for the employer to match anything at all.

But here's what really makes it seem arbitrary: the way the employer can stop a pension plan, or a matching 401(k), or even our health insurance, without notice.

In one case in our office now, we are suing the directors of Outboard Marine Corporation

(OMC). We allege: they cut off the health insurance of 6,000 people, with notice of eight days. Eight! Remember, these men are fiduciaries. Or should be.

Eight days.

Yes, when they did it, OMC was in Chapter 11. Still, OMC had literally millions in assets. They could have given us decent notice. How did it hurt? We had 6,000 people who could have formed their own "group" for health insurance. Much better than paying one by one. But we needed time so we could set it up and roll over our coverage. For God's sake! Some people were about to go in for surgery. Others, chemotherapy. Couldn't they give us more than eight days? But with no notice, we didn't have a chance. I still have dreams about the day-long hearing we had in court, when the judge approved the cut off of our insurance. All day, lawyer after lawyer for OMC or for the banks or for the other secured creditors stepped up to the judge and said:

"Your Honor, nobody likes to do this."
We asked for 120 days. No. 90 days. No. 60 days? No. Finally, like Lot grovelling before God, except without any hope, we asked for 30 days. No.

No. No. NO.

And more lawyers stepped up. Some I see at Democratic fundraisers. "Your Honor, nobody likes to do this."

Or: "Judge, nobody likes to do this."

Or: "Of course your Honor none of us likes to do this."

And the more they said it, the more I thought, They certainly love to say it. And I had the awful feeling that I often get at the end of the hearing: they're going to come over and shake my hand.

I usually warn co-counsel: "Get ready. When we lose they're going to come over and shake your hand." I worry one of the younger lawyers might throw a punch.

No, I'm kidding: lawyers like us never throw a punch.

Later we brought a suit against some of these "fiduciaries." The District Court and the Court of Appeals have made clear they can terminate anything—a pension, health insurance—without even five minutes notice. So part of the collapse of the old trust law is not just that they "can do it" but they can do it in a way that keeps people wondering, minute to minute, if they have any coverage at all.

But it can be worse than losing a pension, health insurance and the like. More and more companies just spin off old units, and set up new ones, in order to bring in younger workers whose insurance costs are less. As I write this (November 11, 2004), I know of two big drug companies which at present are alleged to be doing so. Earlier in the month, a group of workers sued Abbot Labs for doing this very thing. We have also met with about 200 workers at another big drug company, Aventis; they had more or less the same fate. Aventis closed the unit; a manager said it was being closed for good. Then, after the older workers took severance and resigned and signed releases, Aventis started it up again, but now with the younger workers. Why? Our clients think it was to bring in a younger work force that will cost Aventis less.

So people, in their working lives, experience the world as more arbitrary, more unpredictable. No defined benefit. No matching 401(k), and if there is, the little people who are in them are often cheated.

And of course, no health insurance.

And all of it with no notice. The old law of trusts is dead.

I'm afraid it gets even worse. Now the trustees, the guardians, often pick out the weakest of us, the poor, the uninsured, and sue them. I mean our charitable institutions: hospitals, universities. They get huge tax exemptions because they are "charities." They pay no property tax. They have tax-exempt bonds. (In effect, by exempting them from taxes, the legislature appropriates money to them.) Why? To help the "poor," the vulnerable. Presumably, the uninsured: the people whose benefits are cut off. Yet in real life, the hospitals pick out the very ones they are supposed to help and gouge them. Am I being unfair? They charge the uninsured two to three times what you and I, with our insurance, our Blue Cross, have to pay. Two to three times: for a broken arm, a miscarriage. And when the uninsured cannot pay, they come after them in court. Indeed, these charities of old are now like collection agencies. They employ armies of collection lawyers. They phone late at night. "How are you going to pay?" Oh, says a friend, I doubt these hospitals really collect. Of course they collect! They go out and garnish people's wages. It's just my impression, but I think our charities, or their collection lawyers, like to pick on Latinos. A poor Latino family, making $18,000 a year. If they're undocumented, they especially try to pay. For one thing, the charities sue. And they try, and usually do, get defaults. Collection lawyers are careless about serving the summons and complaint. And the poor, terrified, have no legal help. Then the hospitals garnish the wages. Then they try to destroy people's credit. And sometimes, as reported of late in the *Wall Street Journal*, they may even put some into jail.

And this is the new face of the "law of trusts," i.e., the way charitable institutions operate today.

And these hospitals are "charities." Set up exclusively for charitable purposes. But maybe two or three percent of the budget goes to "charity."

Indeed, these new voracious "charities" are partly responsible for our litigation mess. When critics of the right speak of The Legal Crisis in America, they mean, of course, "the Trial Lawyers," people like John Edwards, filing suits against hospitals. The crisis is the subject of a recent *Newsweek* cover: "Litigation Hell" (December 16, 2003). In that issue *Newsweek* gave big play to a Washington, D.C. lawyer, Phillip Howard, author of *The Death of Common Sense* (1995). Howard is a partner at Covington and Burling. His argument in this best-selling book is that there is "too much law," and lawyers and lawsuits are ruining the nation.

Yes, of course, patients sue hospitals without restraint, for everything they can get. I find it appalling. But who started this war? Hospitals and doctors sue their patients far more than their patients sue them. If we simply count up filings, the real litigation hell is the explosion of suits by hospitals and doctors going after patients. In Chicago, many law firms exist just to chase patients: not only to collect bills, but to garnish wages, attack bank accounts. And of course, if need be, to press them into bankruptcy.

Fine, since you don't believe me, let's take "XYZ" Health Care, which I'll call a big not-for-profit charitable hospital chain here in Chicago. At the moment, our firm is suing XYZ for overcharging the uninsured. Just prior to our bringing suit, XYZ was filing about fifty to sixty lawsuits a month against the poor, the jobless, or just working people who were uninsured. XYZ is typical. The number of lawsuits XYZ files per month dwarfs the number filed against it.

When XYZ sues, it seeks two to three times its normal price that the insured pay. By comparison, the plaintiff trial lawyers, when they sue, seem pretty meek. And the trial lawyers do not in fact force doctors or hospitals out of business. But XYZ, and other charities, when they sue, really do push people into bankruptcy. As Professor Elizabeth Warren of Harvard points out in *The Two Income Trap*, the biggest single reason why we go bankrupt is the kind of suits that doctors and hospitals file.

And we now have a total of 1.5 million bankruptcy filings a year!

It is hard to measure all the litigation that the not-for-profits, i.e., our charities, generate directly and indirectly. But who is responsible for the litigation explosion (or so say Phillip Howard and George W. Bush)? The trial lawyers.

In terms of sheer carnage, i.e., in wrecking lives, the hospitals are far worse than the trial lawyers.

But pick up Howard's *The Death of Common Sense*: there is not a word about the hospitals and doctors suing hundreds of thousands of people annually.

So when the patients get the chance to sue the hospitals in return, why should they act with restraint? Of course, it is too simple to say that in the area of medical malpractice, patients are just dishing it back. No, it is part of the culture, I fear. The fact is, the culture is "Winner Takes All." And it is the hospitals, and doctors, with their feverish squeezing of patients, which created the culture in which they, too, are being sued.

How did this happen? In part, one could blame this too on the collapse of unions. For now there are more and more uninsured, or else underinsured—people with deductibles of $5,000 or more. And when the numbers began to grow in recent years, the great charitable hospitals of long ago no longer had the sense they were supposed to take care of them. Not for free, at least. True at one time, as late as the 1950s, many charitable hospitals did provide free care to the poor. But with the passage of Medicare, and Medicaid, it seemed the need for such "charity" or free care for the poor disappeared. Then the cost of health care began shooting up. And with unions gone, employers cut back. Now many of the middle class need some kind of "charity." But the "charity" does not want to go back to providing free care.

These days, the Mother Cabrini type is gone. Her replacement? A CEO making $400,000 and maybe a second salary, though the second one is off of the books. And the boards are full of business guys who are not there to help the poor but to get lucrative deals with the "charity."

But who's the enemy, according to lawyers like Phillip Howard? In the *Newsweek* article, "Litigation Hell," which is a strange kind of homage to Howard, The Enemy of the People is, over and over again, some poor little guy filing a suit.

A kid whose leg was amputated, but it was the wrong leg.

A nurse who claims she was unlawfully fired: age, race, handicap, etc.

And *Newsweek*, in "Litigation Hell," says, in effect: Blame them, not the companies they're suing. And then goes on to pay homage to Phillip Howard. By the way, turns out that *Newsweek* pays a nice chunk of money to Howard's firm. His firm defends *Newsweek* in civil rights suits from reporters whom *Newsweek* has fired. "Litigation Hell" makes no mention of that.

By the way, I hope I have declared my interest here. I am suing XYZ Health Care, one of these charities. Yes, it's a terrible thing what XYZ does: to overcharge the needy, to garnish their wages. The very needy whom XYZ is receiving huge tax benefits from the State of Illinois to serve! But is it the worst case of a charity gone awry?

I fear not.

In America today, the university may be even worse than the hospital. The university is another great charity, or charitable institution, which comes from the Middle Ages. No, I am not about to write in the manner of Foucault. I only want to note: here is another type of charity that is turning into

Frankenstein. It is hard now to believe that even a hundred years ago the typical university was a penniless thing, begging, with barely enough to feed the monks. Now it seems to rival the Standard Oil Trust. Taken as a whole, Harvard and the other Great Universities are on the scale of Wal Mart. This type of charity preys not just on the students or their parents but every one of us, even the very poor. Yes, a Harvard, MIT, or Stanford prey not just on the rich but even on working people. They are tax exempt, so they destroy the tax base of the cities where the poor line up for food from pantries. Of course in the form of bequests and gifts, they get much of the national wealth, tax exempt, for which the working poor also end up paying. They also get financial aid, billions upon billions, directly from the federal and state governments.

Then the university proceeds without legal restraint to gouge people at every income level and way of life. Obviously, students. In most of Europe a student goes to university for free. There is no tuition. So in every developed country but the US (and soon our one ally, the UK), the university does operate in some way as a charity.

True, a kid in Europe often has a civil right to go to college for free. Students here have no such right. Nor do I argue here for such a right. But even under our system, we should have a right to require the university to act as a charity in its dealings with our young.

Let's begin with student loans. Why should a tax-exempt charity be free legally to charge unconscionable tuitions? I am waiting for someone to sue to impose a cap. Is there no limit? It is an injury not just to the student but the taxpayer. The argument for it is: those who benefit should have to pay their share. But this is specious. We, as taxpayers, in various ways, direct and indirect, carry a tax burden that is equal to that of taxpayers in countries where the schools are free. We deserve a benefit, i.e., equal opportunity for young people of talent. Disgraceful enough that even the rich have to pay. Yes, it is unjust even for the rich. They're entitled to the law of trusts as well. But even worse, even incredible in some ways, the middle class have to pay: indeed, not only pay but to have their children take out loans.

Not small loans. Big loans. In other words, indentures that are shaping how our kids will live their lives. It is not just that the universities are cheating these kids; they are cheating the rest of us who pay the taxes too. And remember, like any other American, I am taxed as truly for a Brown or a Stanford as I am taxed in my own state for various public schools. I understand the argument that the kids who go to schools like these should be paying it back, to us, the public, in some way or another. But it's precisely because the kids take out loans that we the taxpayers get so little back. For the kids, understandably, have to pay off the loans. So they veer from public service, or teaching, or lower paying jobs. They go out and prey upon others, just as the university, that great charity, preys upon them. It's because the kids have-to-pay-it-back, that we the tax payers live in a country with little sense of public service.

Little sense of public service among lawyers especially. For typically kids come out of law school with $70,000 or $80,000 in debt. In a kind of hell themselves, these kids have every incentive to spread the hell to us.

For those who really shape the values of these kids are not the people who do the teaching but the ones who chase down the loans. Alas, late in life, I learned a lot about these collection agencies. In Chicago or St Louis or Seattle, you'll find three or four big ones. They fight each other viciously to see who can squeeze the most from kids. So how do I know? I had a suit with one. No surprise: there is a lot of sexual harassment in these places. Some of the collectors are superstars. They make $500,000 or more in "commissions." They're approachable guys, in the sense that they're always in the singles bars. They are the true bounty hunters of the age. And the bounties are big. They want collection fees of up to 25 percent. And because of that, they can get commissions as much as another 28 percent. And of course… they phone… they sue. They can garnish wages up to 15 percent.

Oh I know: they're collecting not for Depaul, or Michigan, but for the Department of Education. But you and I know who ultimately gets the money. And remember, it's the lawyers the bloodhounds of these "charities" hunt down the hardest. The lawyers in turn know how to come after us. It's all summed up in a piece I once read by a man named Roger Roots. He points out that the kids don't sign these loans, there's no guarantee, no co-signer. By any market standard, it's not a loan that makes any real commercial sense. "A student loan is, in effect, a 'mortgage on the debtor's future,' rather than a true commercial transaction."

It's not as if they're taking "payday" loans—though, wait, we'll get to that. In some ways, these things are worse: lifetime contracts of indenture. So faced with these rapacious charities, which want $30,000 or more in tuition every year, some of our best and brightest sign. Which means later on they will be squeezed by "collectors," who seem to crawl up out of singles bars. And maybe they'll be garnished at the office. And stigmatized. Embittered. Some of them will go bankrupt. Even then they often can't discharge the loans.

Who is going to "give back," once they have given back to these schools? As a result, Roots argues, we have more and more inequality. Because as the people at the top have to pay back more, they have to squeeze more from people at the bottom.

The result: the university, like the hospital, creates a culture where people prey on each other, and use the law to take from each other. We see life as more arbitrary and unpredictable.

The system's unfair.

But there is an even bigger way the university has come to prey upon us all. Perhaps in a way more arbitrary than any other I can cite.

I mean the way the university can now patent "breakthrough" drugs, and sell them to taxpayers at monopoly prices. This way, it can make us all beg for our lives. Try to follow the new logic of this kind of "charity": A university is tax exempt so it can do scientific and medical research. In addition, as taxpayers, we also pay it, directly, with grants, to do such research as well. Especially for new life extending drugs. In addition, under the Bayh-Dole Act, the Med School can take a patent on the product of the research. Yes, it's the same research that as taxpayers you and I have funded, already, twice. But now the Med School or the professors can take a patent too. By what legal or constitutional authority do they get a patent, by the way? For under the Constitution, Article I, section 8, the purpose of the Patent Clause is narrow: to encourage "Inventors" to bring their discoveries into the public domain. But we taxpayers have already paid for the discoveries: that is, they are already in the "public domain."

So it would be senseless to let a public charity or its agents, for work we pay for in taxes, twice, to take out a patent as well. But that's what happens. And they license it to the big drug companies. And they charge us to the skies.

Many of the taxpayers who paid to develop the drugs can't afford to buy them. Fearing lawsuits, a few drug companies have brought down the super inflated prices which they charge only to the uninsured. But even at the "normal" prices, the drug barons and universities can go on soaking us. Harvard. The University of Illinois. The University of Chicago. Under the guise of being charities, they plunder America.

Worse is the fact that these charities and their agents can "tax" the very drugs that can save or extend our lives. It is much like the old system of tax farmers and private monopolies in Bourbon France. Think of the tax on salt. But even back then it was not a public charity which did the taxing.

In no other country in the world can the university prey on people in this way—turn faculty into millionaires by this day-in, day-out betrayal of a public trust. In no other country would the public tolerate the way we are tormented by our charities.

Even here, even in America, people may reach a limit as to how much more they can take. Of all the various bodies of law, it's the law of trusts, today, that is most of all in shambles. But there are other candidates.

Chapter Four

From Administrative Law to No Law:
The Rise of the Whistleblower and Trial Lawyer

Yes, I slipped into law school at the very end of the
post-New Deal era. But already kids were dropping
out of administrative law. They were taking trial practice instead. We had already begun deregulating.
Now, instead of administrative law or public law, we
have tort law or private law. We have our private bar,
i.e., the hated trial lawyers, to do what civil servants
used to do. By that I mean the government became
weaker, after 1972. We began wave after wave of
deregulation, and not just of economic regulation, but

even public safety: worker safety; food safety; transportation safety.

There's no reason to learn about the Administrative Procedure Act, because administrative agencies don't do much any more. Now some may object: "Wait, I don't think we de-regulated everything! Maybe we deregulated energy. Maybe we deregulated telecoms. What do you mean, we deregulated safety?"

I know, more liberal hysteria. OK, I am hysterical about it.

It did not always happen formally. It can happen just by defunding regulation. As the great law professor Clyde Summers used to try to teach kids like me: "It costs a lot of money for people to have 'rights.'"

And over and over we gutted the funding of regulation. Think of the deficits since Reagan. Now under Bush. The deficits plot the degree of our deviation from the rule of law. What the numbers tell us is not of any shortfall in entitlements, because legally none can occur. Rather deficits do trigger a shortfall in the execution of the laws. Deficits turn into cuts in discretionary spending, especially for lawyers, regulators, administrative judges. Not to mention the inspectors of worker safety, food safety, automobile safety, drug safety—safety. It's because we regard the rule of law as if it were a free lunch, as if it costs nothing to execute the law, that we fail to grasp what the numbers have to tell us. In a single year it's hard to see. But every year, Congress cuts a little more out of the "discretionary" budget. Fewer people. Less money.

And now to make sure the civil servants don't even ask for money, Congress has started to prohibit unions. But in an era of huge deficits, the effect is all the same: to do less. And not just to do less, but to scare off talented people from public service. Of course with whopping student loans, the ones who used to go into it would have to stay out anyway. We have lost a whole generation of talented people in this way, and now the government itself seems more inept.

Yes, it's hard to see it. But let me give a small example. During the last Bush-Kerry debate, the CBS man asked, "What about the shortage of the vaccine for the flu?" Of course Bush could only mumble. Kerry ducked it too. He talked instead about his plan for health insurance. But I wish Kerry had said, "Yeah, the government screwed it up. What do you expect? We don't get good people in the government any more. Or the ones we have are overworked. Look, if we don't want to pay to have a decent civil service… and by the way, decent law enforcement… this is what we're going to get."

And as we keep gutting the public sector, we'll see panics like this more and more.

Even in my practice I can see over and over the evils of de-regulation, both the open and the covert kind. And since I don't really do administrative law, if I can see these evils, they must be epidemic. Let me pick a few.

Work. The Labor Department, which I know best, seems to me the saddest case. I could pick any office—OSHA, ERISA. But let's take minimum wage. All over the country, people at Wal Mart have been working off the clock, for free. And God knows what is happening in the back, in the smaller places. No one knows.

There's no one in the field to investigate.

It's not the government, but private lawyers who have been bringing suits. Yet the worst cases, we lawyers can't even find. I mean the people who are in slavery. Some of it white slavery. And why can't we find them? Same answer: there's no one in the field.

Once, when I filed a suit to get the Labor Department to enforce the child labor laws for 16- and 17-year olds, kids whom they do not even pretend to protect, I got nowhere. I met with the Solicitor who told me: "Look, suppose I say I agree with you. How would I ever get the money to enforce it?"

He was right. If I had won and they had issued regulations, it would have only been worse. In Labor, as in agency after agency, we have a vast complex body of regulatory law—which would take a mandarin to learn—that no one enforces. The law is "there." On paper. Indeed, it is a lot of paper. How much paper? Fifty volumes, in paperback, in total: I know because I counted. But as to big chunks in these volumes, there's no one to enforce it.

Fifty volumes. What is the weight of that in paper airplanes?

So that leaves it to the private sector, to ordinary citizens, to figure out some way to take the law into their hands. We can't look to civil servants. We look to vigilantes. In particular, we look to trial lawyers, who cherry pick the good cases, i.e., who are in it for the money. Or in the case of many Labor

Department regulations, we look to our working poor, to maids and parking valets, who, we hope, one day, decide to blow the whistle. Do something. Scream. Even if they're fired. What's replaced the civil servant? The whistleblower. Instead of the rule of law, we now have these tiny acts of martyrdom and rage.

Health. Or let's say: patient safety. As I represent nurses, I can see, in this one area, how the rule of law is in shambles. Why?

Hospitals are cutting back on nurses. That's how the hospitals drive up profit margins. Everywhere, the ratio of nurse to patient is ballooning. Patients sit in ERs. It takes longer to start the orders. Oh sure, there are a lot of regulations telling the hospitals what to do. But there are not enough nurses to carry them out. Or civil servants to enforce them. Who knows? There may not be enough trial lawyers to bring the medical malpractice cases! At any rate it galls me to hear the President rail about trial lawyers suing hospitals. Why is it that the trial lawyers bring these suits? Because the hospitals depart from a standard of care, often set out in federal regulations, which the President of the United States has the duty to enforce. And why do the hospitals depart from a standard of care?

Not enough inspectors.

Not enough nurses on the floor.

If the President wanted to cripple the lawyers, he might consider, for example, setting nurse to patient ratios. Of course he won't. Yet as hospitals cut back on nurses, they end up violating more standards and regulations.

Result? More and more patients die. Bring on the trial lawyers! For when the rule of law really is in shambles, that's what people get. When we have no contract, we get tort. And when we have no trust law, we get tort. And when we deregulate, we get tort, as well. One can calculate the rise of tort from the drop in the numbers of those who simply watch over us, from various civil servants to the nurses on the floor.

With the decline in "ad" law, I have become a kind of tort lawyer too. Or at least I run with the vigilantes. Or I file a suit or two for them. I think of P, a nurse who works at Q. Or she did until the hospital fired her. She was a red hot pepper of a whistle-blower. She fired up the nurses. She urged them to file "assignment-despite-objection forms," by the dozens. I-am-working-under-protest-because-there-aren't-enough-nurses-to-cover-patients. And all over the state, yes, the State of Illinois (!), she set up hearings for a Patient Safety Act. And she sent off petitions to get state officials to come look at conditions at the Q Hospital.

Which at last they did.

In other words she is working for us, the public, like a private attorney general. She is doing it without pay, and soon without her job!

When the hospital fired her, I filed suit. Oh, the hospital hates her, calls her a liar, and threatens to sue her for libel. Oh sure, a battle like this is even fun sometimes, I must admit. Like at her deposition. It went on all day. I had a little fun, seeing the way the hospital lawyer dished it out to her—and then seeing the way she dished it back. Both were very good. Yes, at moments, I enjoy an eight hour deposition.

Otherwise, it was just another day in hell.

In any event, is this what now passes for the rule of law in America? It's like a nurse has to pour gasoline over herself and strike a match, to get the attention of a public health official. But there is another area that is even worse.

Safety. Like meat inspection. How could regulation be collapsing here? I am now in a legal battle where we have to prove that the Department of Agriculture bothers to enforce the law at all.

Sound surreal? It sure does. But let me tell you about our suit with the owner of a chicken processing plant. We are suing for his workers under the so-called WARN Act, which requires a notice before a plant closing. In this case, the owner did not give the required 60 days of notice before he closed the plant. "But the Department of Agriculture shut me down," the owner argues. "How could I foresee that?" He argues that yes, he may have done bad things, and let rats run wild, and let rats shit on the chicken meat. And yes, it is even true that the inspectors of the Department of Agriculture gave him "write ups."

But here is the issue: Was it reasonable for the owner to foresee that the DOA would enforce its own regulations?

He had an argument: "I am in the business, and they never enforce the law." Never, never. That was his claim: DOA is more or less a joke. Under Bush I, then Clinton, and then Bush II, it's gotten worse. "Everyone knows!" Now comes the ruling of the district judge, who is a liberal, a Clinton appointee: Yes, he says, it was unforeseeable. It was as if he took judicial notice that as a matter of common knowledge, the government does not enforce the laws. Case dismissed!

I'm still in shock that the employer got away with such an argument. But he had a point. We cut back on inspectors. We don't impose fines. So he had no way of knowing DOA would shut him down. In other words, the application of the rule of law is the equivalent of an "act of God." Like a hurricane. Yes, we appealed. I helped edit the brief. It was not my case, but my colleague's. All I did was to strike out the word "rodent" and put in the word "rat." And the word "rat" came up a lot. For the plant was filthy: full of rats, rat drippings, all over the meat. The scary part was that the plant had gone on like this for years. The more we deregulate, and the more the inspectors are told not to threaten but to "cooperate" and have a "cooperative spirit," the more the rodents, or the rats, are free to go on dripping on our Chicken McNuggets.

So what happened on appeal? Well, of course we argued that a judge cannot assume that it is "unforeseeable" for the laws ever to be enforced. In America, has the rule of law really come to that? Even though we got the District Court reversed, we did not really win the point.

No. We have to go to trial. We have to have a trial as to whether or not the owner of the chicken processing plant has to believe the government when it says to him they're going to enforce the law.

Again, it's not just patient safety or food safety—it's any kind of safety. Lately I have been representing locomotive engineers, and it's even true of rail safety. Rail safety! But people are dying. There are terrible accidents. But we now curb the inspectors!

On November 7 and 14, 2004, the *New York Times* ran two front page stories about how the Federal Railroad Administration is going easy on Union Pacific. Let's be nicer even as the accidents get worse.

And of course here too, we have whistleblowers. I mean literally—the engineers! But they can only blow the whistle if they have a strong union and can keep their federal licenses. As I write, Union Pacific is trying to take away the licenses of a few without the due process which the federal regulations require.

As long as the FRA is going easy on Union Pacific, this will be a tough battle. If the union does not win this, then be careful when you cross the tracks!

Rail safety, for God's sake! How nice if this were just a case of the New Deal in shambles. But now it's a case of the Square Deal in shambles. I mean, the regulatory state as it existed under Theodore, not Franklin, Roosevelt. Sure, I'd like to curb the tort lawyers—as would our President. For I hate to see the law turn into tort. But without the tort lawyers, I might be dead. A train wreck. A spill of deadly gas.

In Chicago, I'm living in a ring of nuclear power plants. I'd be in terrible danger if we tried to curb the tort lawyers. It's only the tort system that saves us from a Three Mile Island. Yes, it might be nice if we had more nuclear plants. We could cut down on Mideast oil. We could slow down global warming. And if I lived in France, with all its nuclear energy, I might think it a good thing. So why do I oppose it here?

Because France has a real administrative state, a real civil service, and the best and brightest do the regulating. In America, we can't even keep the trains on the tracks. And so as a citizen, I'd like to curb our trial lawyers.

But I also want to live.

You may well scoff at the specter of a Three Mile Island, or even a Bhopal, or even, God forbid, a Chernobyl. Perhaps if we curbed the trial lawyers none of that would happen. But consider what happened in one case where we put the lid on trial lawyers.

Corporate Finance. Enron. Worldcom. How did it happen? We got rid of administrative law and then tort law. Then the whole thing blew up. Here is how I tried to explain it, at lunch, to a lawyer friend, Mary M:

> First, in Stage One, we had the SEC, the Securities and Exchange Commission. The New Deal. Joe Kennedy. We got the best, the brightest. We regulated like hell.
>
> Then in Stage Two, we get deregulation. We cut back enforcement. Instead of New Deal, we get Post New Deal Lite.
>
> Then, Stage Three. In come the tort lawyers. With Reagan, they move in. They start to file a lot of class actions, for non-disclosure and fraud. Corporate people say: 'Stop it!'
>
> So fine, in Stage Four we stop it. We get the

Contract with America. Newt Gingrich, the Congress, they pass a lot of laws. We zap a lot of suits. Corporate people are happy.

So then, Stage Five: KA BOOM. Enron. Worldcom. It's Three Mile Island. Everything blows up.

So now, in Stage Six, we have Sarbanes-Oxley. We make the CEOs sign balance sheets with statements, 'I do not engage in fraud.' But is that Mickey Mouse? Yeah. So what is it we really do?

We turn it over to Eliot Spitzer, the Attorney General of New York. A state attorney general, even if the state is New York! He sues the banks, the big companies. I mean, the leading regulator of not just the United States but the whole world economy is now the state attorney general in New York. I like Eliot Spitzer. Thank God for him.

But the Attorney General of one state? Every three or four years we have a new legal paradigm. We get the SEC, then tort, then laissez faire, then self regulation, and then a state attorney general. It's all in shambles.

Mary M paused, and then she said:

"It's like a boiler, isn't it? You try to cap the pressure in one place, and it blows up somewhere else."

Yes, she said it: We get rid of the New Deal, the old administrative law, and now we are about to get rid of tort. Guess what's going to happen? The boiler's going to blow.

Mary's right. What happened at Enron or Worldcom is just as likely to happen in the ER or at a Colonel Sanders or on a rotting railroad track. I hate the way the law is in a meltdown into tort, but I'd rather have a tort than nothing there at all.

If the breakdowns in patient safety, or food safety, or rail safety do not convince you that the regulatory state is now in shambles, and if the legal anarchy in corporate finance is not enough to do it either, then I ask you to consider one final case.

Payday loans. With the payday loan stores, we have gone from administrative law to no law. We hit the bottom. No rule of law at all.

I got involved in a suit against payday loans; otherwise, I wonder if I would have even noticed them. Because of my hero the late Monsignor Jack Egan I got on to a committee to go after payday loans. I ended up filing a suit, which turned out to be mainly a *cri de coeur*. (I mean, we lost.) But let me say what a payday loan is, and why it is such an emblem of the collapse of regulation.

Let's say I'm making $30,000 a year, I have a family, and I'm short 200 bucks this month. I go to you, the Mr. Payday Loan. Now of course I don't literally turn over my next paycheck. But in return for $200, I write you a post-dated check for $240.

I know, you know, and the State of Illinois knows that at the moment I write this check, it is a bad check. It may be "post-dated," but under the revised Uniform Commercial Code, my bank is allowed to cash it now, right away, as soon as I write it.

Right away, I have set myself up. You can prosecute. Now, and certainly later. I can't come up with the money. So to avoid the prosecution, I have to take out another and even bigger loan.

And another.

And another.

I keep writing bad checks, and I keep giving you more and more power to put me into jail. Soon I can owe $1000 for a loan of just $200. Even the Mob with a juice loan hesitates, I believe, to overreach like that.

I have to admit, at the beginning I was annoyed with Father Egan for dragging me into these meetings and paying so much attention to this one little issue of payday loans. Come on! This was a priest who had marched for civil rights. He was a kind of 1960s hero. Isn't there bigger stuff to take on than these stupid payday loans? But it slowly dawned on me what is so awful about the damned things, emblematically.

What is awful and so different from a Mob loan is that the State of Illinois is working as a kind of "silent partner." The state sets up and licenses every lender: We the state know exactly what you're doing. We the state know that you are inducing people to write you a bunch of bad checks. So when you give us the word, we the state will throw these suckers into jail." In other words, the state is part of the scam; it helps induce the poor to commit a crime. In effect it is setting up America's penniless for prosecution.

And the state as a business partner is necessary, because otherwise the payday loan store is subject to a cap. Yes, in the old days, before deregulation, there was a cap on interest. It still exists in Illinois. In theory, the cap on interest here is nine percent! But the cap applies to nothing. Not any more. The state is too weak to apply it to anyone. The banks—yes, the global banks which run the payday loan stores—don't want any cap. They want to charge you and me 20 percent or 30 percent on our Visa bills. And they want to charge the poor 500 percent or 1000 percent on payday loans.

True, in some states there is a limit on the exploitation of the poor. But not in Illinois. And Illinois is one of the better states. It's a blue state. It's liberal. It has a liberal Democratic governor. It has a Democratic state house and state senate. Yet not only is the state too weak to stop the payday loans and the big banks that often set them up, it is often dragged in as a silent partner by the banks to help out with the scamming.

So in this new kind of regulation, we trade in a bit more public trust and get back a bit more private rage. At some level the people know that in the end the state is behind the payday loans. It makes a certain sense, doesn't it? The poor—by poor, I mean single moms, with two kids, at $30,000 a year—go out and play the Lotto, which is a form of robbery by the state. Then, when one day they're short of cash, they go out and get a payday loan, which is another form of robbery by the state.

The deregulation of lending and of everything else in the world is bad enough, and any movement from administrative law to tort is distressing. But mostly these are middle class troubles, how we in the middle class experience the law. Down at the bottom, though, at $30,000 a year and below, the state has not just stepped aside—it is actively engaged in the robbery. (As I write, it is being reported that Illinois is going to cap the annual payday rate—at last—to just 400 percent! It's being considered a "victory" for progressives. What's even worse, it probably is.)

But this is the least of the ways that the poor have experienced the collapse of the rule of law. I now turn to a much bigger one.

Chapter Five

The Deregulation of Public Space:
Or, the End of Equity

One reason the rule of law has collapsed is the retreat
from injunctive relief, or what in law school we used
to call the "structural" injunction. By that I mean the
way federal courts used to order broad changes for
hospitals, prisons, and parks.

Then we cut back this judicial activism. And as
is usually the case whenever legal conservatives
succeed in curbing the courts, it led to a huge explosion of litigation. It certainly did when we cut back on
these big "structural" injunctions. The result? We
went from equity to tort. We went from one big case

for an injunction to a thousand little cases for individual damages.

Example: Suits against the cops. That's one of the big examples in the *Newsweek* special, "Litigation Hell." Too many lawyers are soaking the cities. For what? Police brutality, of course. My own mayor, Richard Daley, is quoted in *Newsweek* with his usual eloquence on the drain of public funds. It seems it costs the city money when the police engage in beatings, the random killing of innocent motorists, and the occasional act of systematic human torture. If torture in Chicago sounds far fetched, you can just read the write ups by our local reporters.

Now prior to the Mayor's statement in *Newsweek*, I had thought the Mayor was in favor of all these suits. A radio reporter had asked him: "Why does Chicago have so many more complaints than New York about police brutality?" And here is Daley's answer, more or less: It's because things are so much better in Chicago. Out here, people aren't afraid to complain the way they are in New York. And if we have more complaints, it only shows our city is better run. People in Chicago have more confidence in the local government.

That's why we lead the country in complaints about police brutality. It's our way of expressing our trust in Mayor Daley.

But in *Newsweek*, he took a different view. He griped about the suits, and how the tort lawyers got too much in damages. Yes, he's right. It does cost too much. I'm a taxpayer, and it galls me to pay even my small share of it.

On the other hand, we "lawyers on the left" tried to enjoin the worst police practices in cases like *Lyons v. Los Angeles Police Department*. Instead of damages in tort, we tried to get court orders to stop the way they treat prisoners. But in *Lyons*, the US Supreme Court, urged on by cities like Chicago, ended the chance for doing that. The Court held that Mr. Lyons had no "standing" to file for an injunction once he had been beaten up and let go. He had no "stake" in a "live controversy," as we lawyers say, at least with respect to future beatings by the cops. How likely was it that Mr. Lyons would be beaten up again? Only a legal conservative could talk like this: "Oh, he has no interest now." It's argued that one-time victims don't "care" any more about what happens in the future. ("Hey, I've already been beaten senseless. This new case has nothing to do with me!") So no one can sue to stop the problem. And if no one can sue, there is no way a judge has the power to fix it. See? Los Angeles won! As a result, the beatings can go on and on. No injunctions!

As a result, the lawsuits for damages can go on and on. And the drain on city treasuries can go on and on. We can thank the legal conservatives. We can thank Reagan. And Bush I. And Bush II. Because of them, we stopped the "legal activism" which could have ended all of this nonsense by an injunction in a single case.

But that's only one little effect—more beatings by cops. We also ended up with more disorder in the streets. We already had enough, just from the rise of poverty in our cities. Yet at this very moment, we are cutting back on judicial remedies—i.e., injunctions—helping to keep some order in our public spaces. In the 1960s, under civil rights laws, federal judges had begun to order cities not only to open up the public facilities to minorities, but to spend money on them.

More money meant they fixed up pools and parks. More money meant they sent in more city workers. And more city workers meant more "eyes on the streets," to use the phrase of Jane Jacobs in *The Death and Life of Great American Cities*. Yes: more money. To fix the broken windows. To make the places nicer. By the mid 1970s, just as the golden age of inner city poverty had started, the courts were issuing injunctions to guard the public space, which meant spending more on the schools, the parks, city services. As Giuliani would later discover, it would have been a good thing if we had fixed the broken windows. But at the worst possible moment, all of this stopped.

We began curbing the injunctions. The liberal judges left. The right now came to power. We could have used the civil law to keep the cities safer. Instead, by scrapping the injunctions, we just got more disorder.

Instead of regulating public space, we deregulated it. As we retreated from this use of equity, we turned to the criminal law instead. It seems from 1980 on that's all we've been doing. It's as if we're trying to put everyone in prison. But paradoxically, by locking up so many, we made the public spaces even more dangerous.

How?

There aren't so many adult males on the streets these days. When we took them away, we ended up spreading the guns and drugs to kids. Thanks to the gangs, which directed things from the prisons, 14 to 18 year olds now took the lead in killing. Of course being kids, they were even wilder, spraying bullets everywhere. By the early 1990s, as more men went to prison, we became more and more fearful about using public spaces. It even had an effect on higher income types like me. After all, by 1993, in my own city the murder rate had reached 95 a month. Even if it's all in another part of town, it's like living in Sarajevo and telling yourself, "Oh it's only another part of the city that is being shelled."

My barber, a young guy, told me the other day, "I dropped out of high school back then, because I was afraid of being killed." It was not just the kids who were scared of being blown away. Even some of my lawyer friends began to notice how many people, albeit in other neighborhoods, were being killed. And it affected the way all of us used the public spaces. People did not feel safe out in the open. Even far, far out, in outer suburbia, we kept our kids entombed in private malls. And in the inner, blue-collar suburbs, it was scary even in the malls.

That's another way the standard of living dropped. Not only in terms of private income, but in our access to public goods as well. Oh yes, the public parks are still there. Even public pools. And there are even public concerts. And we know, "If I decide to use these things, I probably won't be shot." Indeed let's say: "I know I won't be shot."

Yet although I know I won't be shot, somehow the public space is no longer available. Sometimes, it's not geographically available, because I have moved away. But often it is just not psychologically available. Because the rule of law has collapsed in the inner city, public space is just not available to me in the same way it was before.

Who do I blame for the loss of these public goods? I blame some of it on the judicial conservatives, on judges who made it impossible to protect the public spaces. For one thing, they blocked various attempts to stop the spread of handguns, especially to children. When tort lawyers in the 1970s began to sue the handgun manufactures like Colt, the state judges in Illinois and in other states began to carve out special exceptions for the sale of handguns. Really, it was a kind of judicial activism by the right. For handguns, and only for handguns, they came up with rules that existed for no other consumer product. There is a duty of care in the sale or distribution of any product. But the judges decided that this rule of law did not apply to handguns. So? Multiple sales to gangs (through straw purchasers). Mass sales at "gun fairs." The gun industry could do anything.

Principles of negligence that would apply to a company like Coca-Cola did not apply to Colt. And this was not statutory or legislative but a judicially crafted exception, an exception to the ordinary principles of commercial law.

Even without bringing back the liberal Warren Court of the 1960s, we could have used the law to make it a bit safer to use the public space. Or so a few of us who were lawyers in the 1990s thought. And here's my own little story of what we tried to do.

When the murder rate hit 95 a month, I decided I'd join a group of lawyers fighting handguns. And with one of them, Locke Bowman, we cooked up a tort suit, to sue the gun industry for creating a classic "public nuisance," i.e., for interfering with the use of public space. Because now the kids were using guns. People would get shot while sitting on their porches. I wish I could remember who among us said, "Why not sue for public nuisance?" No one said, "Eureka!" But since the courts had decided to gut the law of negligence in the sale of a handgun, the only good idea that we had left to us was public nuisance. It seemed to cry out, medievally, "Give me a try." It was an elderly type of common law. But maybe it could help the kids, who at the rate of 95 a month were dying in the streets. A public nuisance claim is one based on an ancient legal right, the right to use or just perambulate along the public way, and to do so without "interference," without unreasonable "apprehension." Without having to wonder, Should I hit the dirt? It is the right that you or I have to be unimpeded in any way, even by the way that some asshole in a Red State wants to market guns. It is the right to be free of such things as a pig sty or a house full of prostitutes calling out to us, "Come over here and see us!" It is certainly the right to be free of smoke and noise. So why not the smoke and noise of guns, especially when they are being fired at us by kids?

We decided to sue. For Steve Young, whose son had been shot by another kid.

And then for Tony Ceriale, whose son, a young cop, had also died.

And then the city filed a suit as well. Yes, for all my criticism of Mayor Daley, he is my hero when it comes to handguns. And once the Mayor had sued, other cities did as well. Not just the big ones, like New York, but even little ones, like Bridgeport.

Even my hometown of Cincinnati sued!

Here was a chance to use the civil law to protect the public space before it was gone. Maybe, in a small way, all over America, this could create some civic trust. And do away with public rage.

But we lost. The funny thing is, we won at the trial level and the appellate level. Or at least we won the right to sue, to proceed to the taking of discovery, to the depositions. To poke around their house. On this right to proceed, we kept winning, until at last we hit the highest court in Illinois.

In November 2004 the Illinois Supreme Court issued a decision. We lost! The Illinois Supreme Court shut us down, seven to zero. Of course they're elected, and the ones from downstate are understandably afraid of the gun lobbies, the NRA, etc. But we even lost the judges we elected from Chicago! We lost them all.

We lost. Ugh. God, I hate being a lawyer.

All that rainy day, at the news boxes in the Loop, I got to see, over and over, this headline: BIG WIN FOR HANDGUN MANUFACTURERS. "Big win." Just what we need. What a month. Bush is re-elected. And then this ruling.

Don't ever become a lawyer. Six years, gone. Though about the last three or four I have had little to do with the case. Other people have done the work. I dropped out, and they were the ones who were the heroes.

But still, don't ever become a lawyer! Why do people do it?

I still do not trust myself to give a rational and fair reading of the Court's opinion. But there was a special concurrence, from three of the justices, and let me give you the gist, in my grossly unfair rendering:

First, we are sorry about the murders. We really are. It really is terrible. And by the way, not only are we sorry about the murders—the allegations in your complaint are really scary. Wow! Did the gun companies really do what you allege? My God, it probably does violate some kind of law. But you guys can't just come into court like this! We've got a modern regulatory state, you know? Please, you're putting us in a spot. Go to the Legislature! They're elected. Of course, we're elected too, but…

So that's what it boiled down to, in effect: We're just the Illinois Supreme Court. We're just from Illinois. Go away! Go away! All you want to do is scare us!

Oh, I know many will say, "Well, they're right, aren't they? You should go to the Legislature." And I know the other objections: "There are already so many guns out there. What does this suit do about that?" And finally: "Do you really think Congress would let this suit go forward?" Even in the last session, the Congress nearly passed a bill to block these handgun suits. It may still have to pass it, because the public nuisance claim won in Ohio.

Yes, my home town Cincinnati won in the Ohio Supreme Court, but then disgracefully dropped the case.

I know, I know. Maybe it was futile. But let me tell you why I think we should have brought it anyway: To make the judges do what the judges in the Weimar Republic failed to do, to say that murder on the streets is murder. We at least ought to be able to use the courts to make a record of what is going on. The Illinois Supreme Court refuses to let us even do that. "Well, forget this old common law," some would say. "We have the modern administrative state."

But that modern administrative state is also the court. And of course we were not invoking the ancient law, really. We were invoking the way we used injunctions in the 1960s.

We lost. Meanwhile, thanks to their Big Win, the handgun manufacturers will go on selling. The mindless lockups will continue. We have a "modern" administrative state. It goes on locking people up, no matter what the rate of crime. The state is growing: more prosecutors, prison officials, prison guards. Should I mention the other prison-related workers, like the laundry workers or the food service workers, some of them laid off by the airlines? They need jobs as well. These days there is a whole bureaucracy that needs a constant supply of new indictments and prosecutions. Even if the crime rate drops, we have to keep prosecuting about the same number of people.

At least it's true in Cook County.

I sometimes take friends to see Cook County Jail, which is the biggest "plant" or "factory" on the

Side since we shut the mills. When I first came out to Chicago in 1976, the jail had only two "divisions." Now it's up to twelve. In them are mostly people waiting trial. Although the crime rate dropped to a new low, in 2003 the number of indictments hit a new high. We have to feed the Monster: the prosecutors, the cops, even the food service workers who need their county jobs.

Besides, it may well be that the lockup did bring down the crime rate. At least, no one can disprove it. It may always be unclear why the rate did drop all at once in so many different types of cities, from New York to Topeka, all across the land. At some point in the 1990s, it seemed to happen all at once. If the economist Richard Freeman is right as to what pushed the rate of crime up, it's probably fair to say what brought it down: finally, the minimum wage went up. Congress raised it about a year before the drop in crime began. Pushing it up to $5.15 pushed up other hourly wages too, since many wages track the minimum; many companies pay the minimum wage "plus." At least the timing of it works.

Indeed the lockup may have helped push up wages too. When the job market tightened even a little, the wages of the poor shot up—because so many were in jail or prison. That's why welfare reform "worked," or seemed to at first. Otherwise the moms would never have found jobs. Fortunately their husbands and their boyfriends were in prison.

If it pushed up wages, the lockup probably did bring the rate of crime down. Even in Chicago, people are starting to come outside again. We have a big new park on the lake. Parents with their children are show-ing up at outdoor concerts. It's nice. Except, in real terms, the wages of the poor seem to be dropping again, slowly.

And if that's true, children, let's put the chicken back in the picnic basket.

In a year from now we all may be back inside the malls again. I will be curious to find out how many of us, cowering, have been in there all along.

Chapter Six
But We've Lost Our Faith In Juries

Even if the lockup worked, our faith in juries suffered. It is clear that our juries are bungling cases and convicting the innocent. Sure, we have rescued many innocent people from Death Row. But that's because so many journalists and public interest types plunge into these cases. Outside of a Red State, it is sometimes possible to save the innocent from being executed. Some are even led to argue: See, the system works.

But the problem is the system has now "worked" far too many times. It's worked so often that plainly something's wrong. I often wonder whether, with the decline of newspaper reading, people are just getting stupider. Perhaps they're no longer competent to be making these decisions.

It's true. When I was in law school reading the latest Supreme Court cases in Civil Procedure, I used to root for Justice Black, or someone like him, to find a right to trial by jury. I was on the left. I always wanted a jury right. But now, when on a complaint I write "Jury Demanded," I have to ask myself, do I really want one?

For a civil rights or a Title VII race discrimination case, no, I probably don't. Usually a judge is better. For sex or age, I'm not so sure. Let's just say the jury's out.

It's in criminal law that to me, a civil lawyer, the jury system seems so appalling. In part, modern science has exposed the fallacy of folk justice. Every day it seems another DNA test shows how wrong a jury was. In better countries, they got rid of juries long ago. Maybe it's time we should too.

There's yet another way that our big lockup made me lose my faith in juries. It seems as we put more people into prison, we ran out of jurors. We ran out of voters to put on the juries. We had to call on others. Let me explain. Until the 1990s, we used to pick jurors, all jurors, from voter registration lists. At family parties, there is often a loudmouth second cousin who says: "No, I don't register to vote! Hey, that's how I get out of jury duty!" Over the years, the more I heard these people, the madder I got. I wanted to bring a suit to make them serve. To put it as a lawyer might, it is wrong for the state to make a "legislative classification" based upon who does or does not choose to cast a vote. Ah, I wanted to file! But when I talked to a jury commissioner he told me: "Oh no, we stopped taking people for jury duty just from those voter registration lists." The jury commissioners had no choice. Fewer people in America were voting, but more people were committing crimes. Something had to give. Voting kept on dropping. Prosecutions kept going up. What to do? For the first time in history, we began to pull in non-voters, off the streets, so we could keep filling up the jails.

In a sense we were now using "non-citizens" for the most important duty of a citizen. After all these people didn't care enough to vote. So now I was upset. Never mind if it's originally what I wanted when I was going to bring my suit. By the way, how do we get these people who don't register? In many states, the Secretary of State sends each jury commissioner a kind of "master tape." It is a tape of everyone with a state ID, whether a driver's license or non-driver ID. Then the jury commissioner does the canvass.

So we drag them in and make them serve. Once Edmund Burke was able to say that the entire British Empire, with all its pomp and works, existed for only one purpose: to make it possible to swear in twelve men good and true to serve upon a jury. To protect the twelve! He assumed of course they were yeomen, people who cherished a chance to carry out a civic duty.

Now we have to drag them in, impress them like seamen, people who don't even vote or read a paper. The only way we can fill up our juries is to threaten people with jail. Like other lawyers I have seen the judges scream at them: "MADAM! SIR! YOU ARE GOING TO SERVE, OR...."

Yes, I often think that people are getting stupider. But since I'm a lawyer on the left, I am not supposed to say this. Perhaps I can say, the institutions we're "in," or which give us our social intelligence, they are getting stupider. I'm glad people are in churches, since these keep the country from being more atomized than it is, but the church people seem to be getting stupider. Or at least to me, brought up by Jesuits, there's not enough balance of Reason and Faith.

Meanwhile, we're losing other, reason-based institutions, like labor unions. The decline of unionization is also making people stupider.

But maybe my explanation isn't good enough.

Maybe people are just getting stupider—even as more of them are college educated. They don't read. Not the papers. At the same time we have jury instructions not even the lawyers can untangle; some, as I've noted in Title VII cases, not even Descartes could decode.

It's bizarre. So what if they went to college! Why put them on a jury? They don't read, they don't vote. For many people in this country, the first act of citizenship is to put someone on Death Row. The reason I don't want them on the jury is simple: If they experience the world as arbitrary and capricious, then when they get on a jury, they will dish it out to me.

Just try to convince a jury now that what happened to Ms. X is unfair. It's arbitrary. She shouldn't have been fired. Half the jurors are thinking, "That's what you call an unfair firing? That's nothing compared to what happened once to me!" No matter how golden tongued we are, the juries are thinking: I know something worse than that!

I wonder why I keep on writing JURY DEMANDED at the top of the complaint. Still I do, every damn time I file one. As I send it off, I often think, Stop me! What am I doing?

But I go on writing them, the fateful words, JURY DEMANDED. Why do it when I don't want to see a bunch of people who have never read a paper? It's because I'm a liberal, and I'm a Democrat. It's because Thomas Jefferson would expect it of me. Surely Jefferson is dead? Yes. And I do not want to see him, clanking in chains, coming into my room at midnight.

Meanwhile, as people get stupider, one good thing may come out of it: parties are likely to settle without a trial. It's true that if I do not want a jury to decide, say, in a labor case, neither does my opponent, Wal Mart. Who is going to win? No way to tell. Think of the people I could draw.

I could get one of the so-called "millionaires next door," or even three or four of them. I could also get people who should be homeless except that their relatives now take them in. With so much inequality, what's their common bond? Only this: fewer of them read a paper. Fewer of them feel responsible for the laws they will apply.

Even the ones who vote feel no responsibility. For without a one-person, one-vote democracy, even the American people are not responsible for the laws that we apply.

That's a good thing, isn't it? Because juries see the world as more arbitrary, lawyers settle out of court. In a sense, then, the outcomes are more rational. No, I am not conceding that in a paradoxical way, the rule of law is "working." I don't admit it. Yes, some of the outcomes are more rational. But only because We the People are meaner to each other.

Oh, I can still be sentimental about them. I can stand in a line at a McDonald's in a Red State like Indiana, and look around, and think: "This is my country." As I bite into a Big Mac, I can feel one with all America.

But not when I have a client who has something big at stake.

It's too hard to argue a case before people who do not read the paper. It was easy for Lincoln. Back then people on a jury were used to reading whole speeches, reprinted in the papers. They also had all read at least two books. They had a *King James Bible* and *Collected Works of Shakespeare*. Now? Many people now struggle through the captions under the pictures of Britney Spears. For some, even that's too much text.

Lawyers don't want to try cases before these people. Who can blame us? They aren't capable of following an argument. Yes, we settle and the outcomes are more rational. But so what? A decision to settle so as to avoid a soothsayer or a high priest who reads the entrails of a pigeon may lead to a rational outcome. But it would not vindicate a system based on the inner organs of a bird.

There are other ways that the irrationality of the legal system now forces people to settle. For example, the discovery. It's insanely expensive. Now to some it's a puzzle: If the hard or expensive part is over, why not go on to trial? The trial itself is often much less expensive. That is a puzzle.

Yet it's precisely because both parties have large "sunk costs" that no one wants to risk the loss of the huge investments they have made. The more we spend on discovery the more risk adverse we become.

It may seem modern and "liberal" and up-to-date, but the modern trial process really now takes place before the trial. It may not involve entrails, but it is a kind of trial by fire, or water torture, to see which of the two parties during "discovery" can endure the most pain. By the end, both are too traumatized to go on. And with so much money sunk in the case now, neither side wants to submit it to people who have not read a book in years.

But what would I substitute? Not judges, of course. Not the ones I get today. Actually, I like the system they have in Germany. They use a brace of jurors, two only, to sit with the judges, and they do this for a fixed term. It's a type of office.

I wish we had a kind of "merit" selection for jury duty. Possibly I'd limit it to married couples who had been in the Peace Corps in the 1960s. All right I'm kidding. But I am serious that we should have judges interview a group of people, and make appointments of the more sober and responsible to serve for a certain term.

But I have complained too much of juries. For after all, like most lawyers, I rarely see them. If I experience the rule of law as arbitrary, it is not because of the juries but because of the judges I see in court.

Chapter Seven
We Have Lost Our Faith In Judges, Too

So what's new about that? But there is something new.

We, the lawyers, may have lost faith that we can agree on certain common things. We, the lawyers. "The governing class," as Tocqueville called us. I do not mean that we have become cynical about judges. If that were all, it might be easier to have a stable rule of law.

If we were just cynical about judges, we might still think of the law as consistent, predictable. Even if we think, as the legal realists do, "Oh, judges are just acting in their economic interest." If only I had that much faith! At least the law might be more predictable.

Long ago, in a famous book, *The Common Law* (1893), Oliver Wendell Holmes, Jr., a legal realist and a cynic, wrote that, "Law is nothing more than predicting what judges do."

But the problem I have as a lawyer is: How can I predict what judge I'm going to get? As I will try to explain, it's a bigger problem in federal than in state court. When I file in a Chicago federal district court, I could get a Carter, or Reagan, or Bush I, or Clinton, or Bush II appointee.

Let's say there are 21 judges. With seven of them, I could win. With seven, I could lose. With another seven, I could toss a coin. Am I going to be in the court of a judge whose hero is a William Brennan? Or of one whose hero is a Clarence Thomas? In a sense I don't know what "legal system" I'll end up in. Among the 21, I could draw:

- Shadur (Carter)
- Moran (Carter)
- Aspen (Carter)
- Marovich (Reagan)
- Nordberg (Regan)
- Hart (Reagan, I think)
- Zagel (Bush I)
- Gettleman (Clinton)
- Castillo (Clinton)
- St Eve (Bush II)

Never has the rule of law been such a lottery. Nor is it so simple as "Republican" or "Democrat." Sometimes, to make it more of a lottery, a Bush or a Reagan might have picked a moderate. For me as a lawyer, never has it been so hard to "predict" to a client what the law will "be."

How did this happen? Simple. For some time in America, there has been no majority party. Unlike Holmes' day in the McKinley era, or the time of the legal realists in the New Deal era, we are in an era of political deadlock. We have not seen something similar since the Civil War. In 1968, Kevin Phillips wrote *The Emerging Republican Majority*, but in fact no majority has emerged. Neither Republican nor Democrat. No one party rules—or is able to rule for long.

So no one party can pick a bench. Since no one party can pick a bench, there is no coherent single legal culture. Bush I picks his 140 or so. Clinton picks his 140 or so. And Bush II picks his. So isn't that good? We get variety. Perhaps if the two parties were closer together, it might be alright. But they're too far apart. So far apart we now have to use different words to talk to these judges. And the outcomes are really far apart. Not because of the "law" which the judges apply, but because the statement of "facts" in whose brief they decide to read.

Until I actually file the suit, how can I tell the clients if they even have a case?

What has made a single legal culture so impossible is that too many people have dropped out of civic life. We ran out of voters, just as we ran out of jurors. And if there were not enough voters, no single party could be the majority. And if no single party could be the majority, no single party could pick the bench. And no single legal culture could exist.

Instead, we got two legal "benches." Or two "cultures," each out to undo the other's "rule of law." I really do think of it as two separate court systems. And it's not that I'm thrilled to be in the Carter-Clinton culture. It would be nice to say that thanks to Carter (left), then Reagan and Bush I (right), then Clinton (left again), then Bush II (right again), we now had a simple split of left and right. If only I could say so! But there is no left or a bench of the left. Like Carter, Clinton did not appoint lawyers on the left like his old friend Peter Edelman, or his class-mate, Lani Guinier. He did not, or could not, because the Senate would have blocked him. Clinton did not have the "political capital" to spend.

So by two benches or two cultures I mean moderate right (like David Souter) v. the extreme right (Antonin Scalia). Or I mean the American Bar Association v. the Federalist Society, the right-wing legal group founded in 1982. The "left" is the ABA which in any other time in our history would be the bastion of the right, like in the William Howard Taft era. The new right, the Federalist Society, is far to the right of this old right.

How so?

I could say: they think government is illegiti-mate. But it's really worse than that. They think everything is arbitrary and illegitimate. It's all subjec-tive. When people like me talk about the good and true, they stick out their tongues at us. Others just cover their ears.

"That's just your opinion! We don't want to hear you moralizing!"

And then like Moses in the Old Testament, they raise up the Ten Commandments, i.e., the truths of liberalism, and smash them on the rocks. "STOP MORALIZING!"

"The Equal Protection Clause? Bah! That damned Lincoln must have drafted it. It's just an excuse for all the liberal judges to moralize."

"The Declaration of Independence? Ugh! Who says these truths are self-evident? They aren't evident to us."

"The Geneva Convention? Ah, that's all political! In these little Third World countries, they just want to tell us what to do."

Perhaps the world seems as arbitrary to these often young lawyers on the right as it does to some of my old blue collar clients who now go down to the riverboat casinos. I like to imagine these old guys driving past the University of Chicago just as the kids in the Federalist Society are holding a meeting. They could stop and tell the kids how they lost all sorts of rights. They could really tell the kids that in our so-called rule of law, there are no fixed or settled meanings.

That's the big difference between the old ABA right and the new radical right. We on the old ABA right are old fogies in spats. Some of us really do think: Oh, some truths are self-evident. Don't ask us which ones, though.

We're old. We're out of it. We clap politely when someone mentions *Brown v. Board of Education*. But the new right is young. Hip. The Federalist Society is full of kids. They don't believe anything has a settled meaning. And when they talk about things like the Constitution, they like to use the equivalent of potty language.

A small example: the dissent by Clarence Thomas in *U.S. Term Limits et al. v. Thornton* (1995). It's when I read this dissent that I really woke up. In *Thornton* the issue was, can a state legislature impose term limits on US Congressmen who happen to be in districts in the state? At one time in our country, this would have been an easy case:

No. A state legislature can't vote a congressman out of Congress.

Yet while that's what the Supreme Court decided too, it was a close one, five to four. Four Justices signed a Clarence Thomas dissent claiming that Arkansas or any other state can override even the US Congress in deciding who can sit in Congress. But it's not just the main argument that woke me up. It was the kookiness in Thomas' footnotes and asides. For example: "We the People"? It doesn't mean "We the People of the United States." Is that what you thought? The Founders really meant, We the People of Virginia and We the People of New York and so on, and not We the People of the United States. Why didn't the Founders write out all the names of the states? Maybe they didn't fit. Clarence Thomas even wonders if it is correct grammatically to use the United States as a singular noun. Maybe we shouldn't say, "The United States is Number ONE!" Maybe we should say, "The United States are Number One!" As well as Number Two! And so on down to Number 50. And the bigger point to which all of this leads Thomas and the other justices: It is not We the People who are sovereign. How can sovereignty be in the People of the United States? There is no such thing as the American people, singular.

Then what's left? We the People of Arkansas. We the People of Virginia. All the others. The fifty Peoples of the fifty states are the sovereigns. If that sounds like an argument for secession, it should. For Thomas' dissent more or less quotes here from the work of John C. Calhoun. Yes, Calhoun! The Senate champion of slavery, the rival of Henry Clay and Daniel Webster. That's the gaunt old man the dissent is quoting: Calhoun—who made the case for secession!

Not that I would have caught it. My old college professor pointed it out. "He's quoting Calhoun."

"You mean an African-American Justice is quoting Calhoun?" I said.

"It's a little odd, isn't it?"

Remember, Calhoun's the one who wrote, "Not everyone is entitled to liberty." Maybe Thomas will quote or paraphrase that too one day if and when he decides the Thirteenth Amendment is unconstitutional. Did a true majority in South Carolina agree to it? The dissent really woke me up. Until then I thought we on the left just had to defend the New Deal. I was wrong. From then on I knew we had to defend the Union, too. Not just Lincoln, either. We had to defend Hamilton and Madison and their idea of a national government in *The Federalist Papers*.

That's what Clarence Thomas and his right-wing law clerks are against or think that they're against.

Now it may sound odd for don't the kids say they are members of the Federalist Society? Yes. And sometimes they quote the Federalists with approval. But mostly they attack them. They quote the Anti-Federalists, who wanted the Articles of Confederation.

But the Anti-Federalists, such as Patrick Henry and George Mason, who opposed the Constitution, didn't go far enough. Calhoun, who came later, in the 1830s, is much more an intellectual's intellectual. He is a lot hipper. He is like a postmodernist who favors slavery. He likes to write and take words and show that everything can be turned upon its head. Yes, even "We the People."

And my old professor told me that on campuses there were kids who described themselves as "neo-Calhounians." I began to have nightmares about Calhoun. In my sixth-grade history book he looks a little like the grandfather of Lucifer. I can see Calhoun in some of the drawings of Blake. And it was Calhoun in absentia to whom Andrew Jackson raised his glass and made his famous toast:

"Liberty and Union, now and forever, one and inseparable!"

I think I mixed that up. Maybe that's what Daniel Webster said. Anyway, Calhoun, carried into the Senate on a cot, was an old coot, but smart. To defend slavery, he knew he had to show that we liberals were frauds. "Moralizers."

And the meanings we attach to words like "We the People" he, in his pomo way, would cleverly deconstruct.

But maybe I make too much of it all. It sounds like these neo-Calhounians just believe in state rights. Aren't I making it too complicated? Yet here's the "neo" in the neo-Calhounians. They don't really believe in state rights either.

What's new about the new right is they don't care about the states. I'd say it's even true for the old right, people like Rehnquist who may once have been a genuine state's-righter. But for many on the new right, some of the states are terrible places, little over-sexed lands of Gog and Magog. The states stand in the way of the culture wars they'd like to bring.

And so, many in the new right are now turning on the states. At least, they don't want any rights for the Blue States. Not the states that expose the nation to: gay marriage; gay rights; assisted suicide; even suits against handguns.

And apart from the religious right, the business right now sees that a state attorney general like Eliot Spitzer can hit them harder than the feds do. In state courts, lawyers can bring class actions for not just millions but billions of dollars. In the case of tobacco, they seek even hundreds of billions of dollars.

Why still be in favor of states when the new right now controls the nation-state itself? In part because the Constitution tilts to minority bloc rule, the new right at the moment seems impregnable at the national level. At the same time, it is hopelessly out of power in many of the states. It has been far easier in fact for the new right to thrive at the national level than to take over in America's big and wealthy states, like Illinois, California, or New York. As I will rattle on about below, our national government is not all that accountable to the majority. There is no one-person, one-vote. That's partly why so many people in America give up on voting. Since about 1962, though, when the Supreme Court decided the reapportionment cases, every state government has operated on the principle of one-person, one-vote. That's when the right slowly began to lose its ardour for state rights. As a New Dealer type, I don't like the states much either. But I have to admit that in the last fifty years the states have become more or less true republics while the national government has become less and less so. Yes, even a Red State like Texas, or Florida, is more likely to do something like raise the minimum wage than the federal government is.

Hence, it makes sense for the new right at the national level to clamp down on the states. In many bills in Congress—assisted suicide, gay marriage, pre-emption of state class actions—they are doing exactly that. But if they turn upon the states, what do they believe in? At least the old right believed in the sovereignty of the states.

Can the new right? No. They have to murder their darlings.

So that's why they are such moral relativists, and why some of them now tiptoe into nihilism. Right in front of our eyes they are turning their value system upside down.

Well, goodbye state rights! Not that the kids who clerk for Clarence Thomas care. To them, it's just a game. It's the older ones, like Ashcroft and Rehnquist, for whom I feel a little sad—just a little. I'm sad for Rehnquist, anyway. Long ago, as a young Justice, he put his heart into a little revolution, to build up the immunity of the states from federal law. In the 1970s, in cases like *National League of Cities v. Usery* (1976), he tried really hard to treat the states like real sovereigns. He tried to exempt the states, or state employees, from any type of federal law. Age. Handicap. Civil rights.

Suddenly, he's backed away. Recently, the Court ruled, with Rehnquist, that the Family and Medical Leave Act did apply to the states and their employees. What? I heard a talk on this by a law professor. "Oh," she said, "it's because Rehnquist has a daughter, a single parent, with a kid, and he's really concerned about his little grandchild."

See? A little child shall lead them.

Well, maybe. I'd bet, though, that Rehnquist, sick at heart, has come to see that he and the right have to turn their fire on the states. Look at Attorney General Ashcroft arguing in the last year of his tenure that federal law pre-empts a state like California from allowing people to smoke pot. It's only for "medical purposes," whatever that means in California. The day of the oral argument in this case, the *New York Times* ran a big editorial to the effect: PROTECT STATE RIGHTS!

But the original purpose of state rights was to let us own slaves. Now it seems to be to let the states get stoned. At any rate, if the left can quote Calhoun as well, then it must seem on the right that the rule of law is now in shambles. They have no real jurisprudence, no neutral principles any more. The right is much more dangerous when it is unmoored like this, with nothing to believe in.

I doubt that the kids in the Federalist Society ever believed in this old right stuff anyway. They don't care about state rights. They go to Harvard, Yale, the University of Chicago.

Do they believe in state rights? No. I doubt many of these kids can even shoot a gun, or could hit the back of a barn.

So what does fire them up? It's not that they hate D.C. or the states. Or hate government as such. They just hate us, the liberals, and all our little pieties. That's why they quote Calhoun, and use potty language, constitutionally.

Why have these kids turned on us, their liberal elders?

I hope it's simply that the right is paying money. After all, many of these kids actually love government. Like the young Dick Cheney, they want to do public policy. Along comes Mr. or Ms. Federalist. "Well, how would you like to work on a Really Big Issue?" "Hey! Sure, cool." In another era, they might have been liberals. Then the right came along and began handing out the candy.

Also, I like to think these kids don't really believe it matters what they do. After all, we have had decades of divided government. There is no real majority rule. Nothing ever really changes. Nothing we do or they do will ever have any consequence.

But here's what I hate to think: I hate to think that we on the left have taught these kids to be on the right. I fear we may have inculcated them with some

(not all) of our moral values. Our relativism.
Scepticism. Our own dislike of certain kinds of
moralizing. What seems to me so different about the
kids in the Federalist Society is the way they use our
own arguments against us. They use the intellectual
weapons of the left against the values of the left. "You
taught us everything was relative. Fine. We apply the
point to you. You want equal protection? Equal for
whom? You're against torture? Whose idea of
torture? We the People? Who are the People?"

That's why I'm fascinated by the Culture
Wars in the schools. Here, on the left and right, we
line up in such a different way than we do in the
courts. In the courts, we on the left believe in the
moral absolutes and the angels of our better nature.
Jefferson, Lincoln. In the courts, people on the right
like Bork take the side of the prison guards and even
torturers and say that everything is relative.

We sound like the high church. How easy for
the right to shock us. So it is with the memos on
torture. All the young Federalist lawyers, in the
White House and the Pentagon, working on these
memos. Yes, they're so top secret. What a scandal
when we find them. But the whole point is, they want
us to find them. Otherwise, why would they even
bother to write them? I know, it makes no sense, but
they care more about shocking us than about tortur-
ing the detainees. It would take a Dostoevsky to
explain it.

Now I admit, I am describing the new right at
its worst. Even the Federalists, even these kids, have
moments of rationality. Even a Clarence Thomas.

And on the right, I should add, there are some judges who are grown ups. Being on the bench and dealing with a docket of three hundred cases has a way of helping to achieve that. I can't say, some-of-my-best-friends, etc. Yet as a lawyer I can say, there are some Republican-appointed judges I'd rather be before than some of the Democrat-appointed ones.

Why? After a while, some judges run out of sympathy for the parties with whom they are "supposed" to sympathize politically. It happens often on the left. Yet it also happens on the right. One day a judge might wake up on the wrong side of bed and think: "I'm sick and tired of collection agencies."

Just as liberal judges get sick of hearing from widows and orphans, sometimes, even on the right, they can feel the same way about banks and lenders.

Sometimes.

Anyway, we have to have a right. I know that. What is scary about this "new" right to me is the way that lawyers are making a cult of attacking not just justice or even morality but human reason. Do I exaggerate? Perhaps. Yet look up the speeches that a Bork or Scalia give. It's a disgrace the language they use, especially in front of students. Alas, I wish I had made a list of the most scandalous talk. But I remember some. Bork, in a famous speech, in 2001, said that whenever people try to use law to stop crimes against humanity, it made him feel "nauseous" or "somewhat nauseous." It's the kind of talk one would expect from a Goebbels. And Scalia is just as bad: scoffing at moral values of every other country and denying that even universal moral norms ought to be the norm in ours.

Yes, it's true, in attacking universal norms of morality Bork and Scalia are only being moralists. They are in a moral rage against those who "moralize." Like Moses they smash the Ten Commandments. Thou shalt not act on moral values! But if we are not to act on moral values, what is the way we should behave?

Here is where they invoke in a perverse way the Doctrine of Original Intent, i.e., to interpret the Constitution as the Founders intended originally. In the case of abortion or gay rights, we should interpret the Constitution to do in 2005 what the Founders intended to do in 1787. But what did they intend in 1787 for us to do in 2005? Even to ask what the Founders intended to do about gay rights verges on absurdity.

All the better then! The new right relishes absurdity. Here is the real break of the new right from the old right. The new right is not interested in ancestor worship or tradition. Many of them hate the Founders, actually. The new right is looking for a way to reinforce the notion that the world is arbitrary and absurd. For the new right what is illegitimate is to use our human reason. Sometimes they may also try to mock us by invoking "majoritarian" values: "If you don't like it, why don't you liberals just amend the Constitution?" But the Constitution is set up to preclude that kind of thing. It cannot be amended by any majoritarian means. The new right knows this of course. To amend takes three quarters of the states. That means, in real life, an amendment requires the approval of state legislatures accounting for 96 percent or more of America's population base. Of course that's an absurd undertaking, no matter how strong a majority movement. The new right takes a certain pleasure in the absurdity. See? It shows the world is arbitrary. Let the Constitution be our tomb. Let it be a kind of death pact among the fifty states. Let the Founders who sought to free us turn out to be our jailers now instead.

Original Intent ends up frustrating Original Intent. The Original Intent of the Founders, who were children of the Enlightenment, is that we stand on our own two feet as adults. But now it is being used to keep us in what they would regard as a kind of perpetual childhood.

The flaw here is to explain the Founders' first order intent in terms of their second order intent. The issue of what in 1787 they thought the Constitution should do about gay marriage is one of a second order intent. The issue of what in 1787 they thought we should do about gay marriage in 2005 is one of first order intent. Their first order intent was for us to use reason. In doing so we should use it as they did, to take the best practices of other countries and adopt them as our own.

What's insidious about Original Intent is the way it is morphing into an ayatollah type thing. It is not "moralizing" they want to stop; rather they want to stop us from thinking. They would stop us from using what the philosopher John Rawls called our "public reason." That's what they want to stop.

Stop thinking.
Stop talking.
Stop. Stop. Stop.

As more of the new right get on the bench, more will rail at any talk of a higher moral norm as making them "nauseous" or "somewhat nauseous." This does not bode well for the future of the rule of law.

Chapter Eight
So What Is Our Judicial Philosophy?

Our judicial philosophy? That's kind of a puzzle.
What do lawyers on the left believe? We are a little
disoriented ourselves. After all, the Constitution is a
blank. It smiles and keeps its secrets about matters
which a modern constitution covers. We suppliants
come and beg it to say something to us about health,
or education. Speak! But this Dead White Male thing
lies there lifeless. Why can't it speak?

Because we cannot amend it to decide
anything, we end up experiencing the rule of law as
arbitrary. Think of *Roe v. Wade*. The right has a point
in saying that *Roe* is not legitimate. Let us put aside

that in the Constitution, there is no right to abortion. There is no right to privacy either—from which *Roe v. Wade* could be derived, maybe. It would seem *Roe* is illegitimate. We have tried to settle the issue without any consent, without any legal norm, or at least one in the Constitution. The people on the right are correct to be outraged.

It's odd, on the other hand, that *Roe*'s been like a rock. It is the only constitutional law or principle that really has been rock-like or fixed, since I got out of law school. Typical, of course, that the only law we have which is like a rock is a law that says there shall be no law.

The people against *Roe* end up experiencing our rule of law as arbitrary. That's bad. They rage. They rant. They would tear down the rest of the legal system. They do tear down the New Deal. Some or even most of them do it in a stupor. They're so mad, beating their tom toms over *Roe*, they fail to see that they are in debt, that they shop at Wal Mart, that they have no health insurance, no pension.

But they hate *Roe*!

OK, *Roe v. Wade* is constitutionally illegitimate. There is no right to privacy in the Constitution. Not a word. But if there is no right to privacy, then maybe the Constitution is illegitimate. That is what the critics of *Roe* fail to grasp. If *Roe* is not legitimate, because the Constitution has no right to privacy, then maybe it is the Constitution which is a problem.

How can we have a Constitution with no right to privacy? To repeal *Roe v. Wade* because the

Constitution never did have, and never will have, a right to privacy, is to force many to conclude, maybe the Constitution is illegitimate.

It cannot be amended. It cannot be brought up to date. Except if we close our eyes and say there has to be a right to privacy, there is nothing in the Constitution on which one could hope to base a *Roe v. Wade*, whatever you may think about the right to abortion.

There is no "there" there. And there is no way to put anything "there." How nice if we could update it, but we who live under the Constitution have no hope to amend it. There are only two even conceivable ways:

1. Have another Civil War, or War between the States, and get the Blue States to impose it on the Red States, or vice versa.

2. Get unanimous consent from everyone, like in the Polish Diet of Nobles in the Middle Ages. I say "unanimous" because it would take only one quarter of the states representing six percent of the US population base to block an amendment to the Constitution. Only 12 states are enough for a veto.

Little states, Red States, states where the Unabomber and militias live.

That's a big reason why we experience the rule of law as arbitrary. Oh sure we can amend the Constitution to make a few technical fixes. Presidential term limits. The voting age. But we cannot address any serious matter. As the centuries slide by, the Constitution becomes ever more dottily out of date.

Every other constitution in the world is more up to date than ours. In Europe after 1945 they all got new republics, with hot-from-the-printer constitutions. In Asia, the newly independent countries got them, too. They have a right to health care. A right to employment. And most of the other rights set out in the United Nations Universal Declaration of Human Rights. Other nations, like Uganda, take up the rights of women and children. Some address the environmental crisis we all are facing.

What does that mean?

First, they have norms, in writing. Second, they have consent. Or a legal system to which, in recent years, they have given a real popular consent. We have to pretend: oh the Framers! They are so wise. Who are we to give our consent?

We the People already gave their consent. Unfortunately, all the people who were We the People have been dead a long time. It is hardly their fault if the ice caps are melting and we cannot even imagine how we'd ratify a treaty on global warming. What do we do? We Americans seem to function as one another's jailers. The Constitution is like a cage from which not one of us can escape. Except in one way— alas, it's through the courts.

I know—no one likes to say that. "It's so elitist!" People should go to their legislators, etc. "Let's have majority rule!" But it's precisely because we have no majority rule that we have to use the courts. Throughout our history we have often asked the courts, "Please do what we would do for ourselves if we had no Senate, no Electoral College, no 50 states."

Please do what we as a country would do if we had majority rule.

Since we have no majority rule, it is hard to guess what we would do. It's doubly hard because if we did have majority rule, it would change us. We would be more like the people in other well off countries. More like Canadians or Europeans.

That's been the puzzle of the lawyers on the left. We look for some external, objective standard: This is what a majority, acting rationally, would do if we had majority rule. This is what the Federalist types of today want to stop.

That's why in the 1960s some of us in law school were reading people like John Rawls. He was not a lawyer, but a philosopher. He was shy, nice, and thin. He danced with the angels upon the heads of pins. He wrote a book, *A Theory of Justice* (1971). When I was in law school, it was a wonderful thing to own. It was not just a book, but a kind of totemic thing, which some kids would covet, had to "own," because they wanted to have "a theory of justice." Well, Rawls did not write as well as the right. But at least he did not write things like, "Human rights make me puke."

He was the opposite of a Bork; he was incapable of a tort.

But he had a love of contract. He wrote about a social contract. In effect he tried to come up with the type of contract that as rational people we would enter if we did not have a Constitution. He did not argue, as we on the left might argue now, for natural rights or human rights. Deep down, he may have believed in these things. But he tried to figure out from our self interest alone what we as human beings ought to do. Let's say I am in the State of Nature or in the Original Condition or Position. And now in the United States, I am to be dropped into someone's house at random. Not knowing where I would land, what kind of income inequality would I want? I won't go through it all. His answer—we want a little but not too much.

Now in the Constitution there is an Amendment that calls for "Equal Protection." Could we not think about the meaning of it the way that Rawls would? That's what we were debating in the 1960s. In the end, many of us realized that to figure out how much equality we would want was just too hard.

Though Rawls meant it to be an objective calculation of one's self interest, it turned out to be a pretty subjective thing. Poor Rawls! I sometimes think he dropped out of favor because of a Supreme Court decision in a single case. In 1974, soon after Rawls' book came out, the Supreme Court decided *Rodriguez v. San Antonio School District*. In that case, the plaintiffs raised to the Court the very issue Rawls did. They challenged the use of the property tax to pay for the public schools. Some districts were rich. Others were not. In the distribution of money for these children, how much inequality did we want? It all seemed to come out of Rawls' book. Some of our professors caught their breath. This would be the Big One. It would decide whether we on the left could litigate the fairness of income distribution. In my adult lifetime, this may have been the biggest Supreme Court case. How did the Court come out?

We lost. But it was close, 5 to 4. In other ways it didn't seem we'd lost by much.

Yes, the holding was: Texas could screw the poor. Or deny them equal funding. The poor, unlike racial minorities, are not a special class. If the Court started to help the poor, where would it end? There was no "standard." In effect the Court was saying, "There was no right to education in the Constitution, even if there should have been." The Constitution otherwise was just too vague. It was hard to know how much equality there should be.

Still, the Court urged us to be cheerful. Even in a state like Texas, equality was increasing. As the Court noted, in Texas in the 1960s there was more and more parity in school funding. Things would get better. Though it's hard to believe now, once upon a time in America equality—even in income—was increasing. Maybe we did not need Rawls or his ideas about justice as fairness.

Unfortunately, we did.

At the time the Court decided *Rodriguez*, inequality in income began to explode. Now I despair that we can use the courts to redistribute, to argue for Justice as Fairness. The gap in income has simply gotten too big. In income, in health care, in schooling, in voting—everything is getting worse. Look at funding of the schools. In my own state, Illinois, the gap in school funding is now about $4,000 per pupil in the poor districts to $15,000 or above in the rich ones.

That's the gap now in Illinois, a Blue State, just in public education! It's worse than in Texas 40 years ago.

There is no way for Rawls to be of help now. Ever since he wrote that book, it's as if someone with a voodoo doll put a hex on his whole approach. As I say, the inequality is now too great for any hope that a lawsuit can make a dent in it. How can we ask a judge or any other member of the elite to even guess what is justice or fairness? Our brains are too addled by the inequality we enjoy.

We simply cannot fix the rule of law in this way. We cannot ask the courts to figure out what kind of justice we would have if we all acted rationally under conditions of majority rule. So what does that leave?

We could instead seek majority rule itself. We could go back to the old Warren Court project, based on the fourth footnote in the *Carolene Products* case, to expand the opportunity for people to vote. I doubt that we could change the Constitution in any formal way. But we could change the "unwritten" Constitution, in informal ways, by state law and court cases, to get the voting rate in the country up to 70 percent or more.

To keep people from experiencing the rule of law as more and more arbitrary, we have to change how we vote. And at least in part we have to go through the courts.

I know, there is much groaning about how the left is always going into court. "Let's stop trying to win our victories in court, instead of at the polls." I have two answers. First, the left rarely wins in court. The central fact of American history is that the left gets clobbered in the courts. I speak as a union-side labor lawyer. Over and over, from 1830 to now, the courts have enjoined strikes, smashed unions, and made it impossible to organize. In our own era, the courts have made a hopeless tangle of the Wagner Act. It is because the left does so terribly in court that there is no socialism in America. Also, no social democracy. Also, not much of a Democratic Party either.

Yes, we did get civil rights through the courts. But it was not the left but the government that used the courts to push the civil rights revolution.

Yet it is true that from the 1940s through the early 1970s the left did win a few victories in court, and it is instructive in what way it did win. It won, and is most likely to win again, when it used the courts to expand the right to vote. And if we expand the right to vote, then other rights not related to it tend to follow.

The right to join a union.

The right to health care.

What proof do I have? That these rights arise inevitably in every country with a constitution, written or unwritten, that delivers a sufficient degree of majority rule.

All the liberals on the courts had to do was to let The People be the people. Let them vote, and vote, and vote. Extend the right to vote and the right to "majority rule" as they never had been available to the American people before.

That's the second reason I think we should go into court. It is legitimate to do so, and no one can fault us, if our only reason for doing so is to expand this right to vote. There has never, never been a back-lash against the left for doing so.

Now some reader may say: "Wait, I don't remember the left going into court to expand the right to vote. Are you sure this really happened?"

It did happen. It started in 1938, and it picked up in the post-war era as Europe and Asia were writing their new constitutions. It was our way of being part of the same global movement. And it almost worked. Through the courts, we just missed by a whisker getting enough "majority rule." But since even some lawyers don't remember it, let me pause here for a moment and quickly tell the story.

In 1938, after Roosevelt tried to pack the courts, the Supreme Court decided to give up. "OK," they said in effect. "We won't go on knocking down all these left-wing laws." Or even bash unions for a few years. But if the Court didn't knock down left-wing laws and bash unions, what was its job? After all, the Court has to knock down something. So when it gave up in 1938, the Court dropped a little footnote, in a certain case. It was the *Carolene Products* "footnote 4." This footnote tried to answer the question: "Well, now what are we going to do?"

And it was written by Justice Stone's law clerk. Here was a kid unknown today who more or less changed American history. He wrote in effect, "Look, we aren't going to frustrate the majority any more. In fact, we're going to do the opposite. We're going to save judicial review for two big things.

"First, we're going to knock down laws that 'restrict the political processes which bring about change…' You want majority rule? We're going to give you majority rule.

"Second, we're going to knock down laws aimed at 'discrete and insular minorities.' In other words, one of these days, we're going to get rid of Jim Crow-type laws."

My rendering is a bit loose. But that's the idea. It's almost out of a Greek tragedy, how the nine Justices who had been the Furies would now turn into the Eumenidies and bless, instead of rage against, majority rule. This whole rationale for this new judicial review is laid out in a wonderful book by John Hart Ely, *Democracy and Distrust* (1980). I urge everyone to read it! As Ely and others have pointed out, the two goals in footnote 4 are really the same: more "participation." Alternatively, I would say, footnote 4 means We the Court are going to let more people vote. Not just white people but black people.

And not only are they going to vote, but there's going to be a lot more majority rule when this is over. And while footnote 4 doesn't say so, it was a way of updating our Constitution. Make it more like that of a European-type social democracy. They the People would put in the right to vote, the right to health care, and all the other rights they need.

And who knows? It might have worked. Look at the 1960s. The People almost did do it, and the Court was a big help. First, blacks began to vote in huge numbers. In cases like *Brown v. Board of Education*, the Court helped discredit Jim Crow with the legal community and make it easier for the civil rights marching that was to come. Second, the states at last had majority rule. In cases like *Baker v. Carr*, the Court put in one of the biggest "constitutional" changes in American history: i.e., one person, one vote. Now the states had to have real majority rule, at last.

By the 1960s, the Court under Earl Warren declared that voting was a "fundamental right." The Court struck down poll taxes, changed voter registration, and pushed one-person, one-vote at the local level. It also made it easier to vote in party primaries. Of late I've wanted to give up on labor law to do voting rights. I've read these old cases. At times, it is shocking how far the federal courts went. A court in the South held that illiterates had the right to make the state help them fill out their ballots. A court in the North held that Puerto Ricans had a right to vote in Spanish. People awaiting trial had a right to vote in jail! The state had to provide absentee ballots.

By 1970, the courts had pushed up the voting rate. Other things, like the Voting Rights Act, helped. But the courts vigorously pushed the Act. The courts got in black voters. By knocking down the poll tax, they also got in more whites. And they clearly made state governments much better than before.

In a sense, they did "amend" the Constitution, in an unwritten way. Was it legitimate for them to do so? In any other country, the question would be unnecessary. But our Constitution does not encourage We the People to participate. Right-wing judges argue, "Where in the Constitution is there any right to vote?"

For the left, nothing could be better than to have a big argument over that. Still, a right to vote is hard to find. Even more, the right of a majority to rule. Remember the checks and balances. The two senators per state. And remember *Bush v. Gore* in 2000. You and I think, well, there must be the right to vote, and there must be majority rule. So we think. But some of the more right-wing Founders would be appalled.

OK, so what? Nearly all the right-wing Founders were disgraced and out of office in just a few years. Never forget that Jefferson got rid of all of them.

Nor do they have any right to impose on us minority rule today. Even the right in this country likes to taunt the left, "You have to work through the majoritarian political process." Fine. How do we "work through" such a "majoritarian" process if no right to majority rule exists?

So from 1938 to about 1975 the Court did try to slip in where it could a bit more majority rule. But footnote 4 could only take the Court so far. Maybe at some point it had to hit a wall.

By the 1970s, people were dropping out. Despite everything the Court did, the voting rate began falling. Now it's at an all-time low, at least in the North. It did go up a bit in 2004. Only in America would people on the left (on the left!) go around ga-ga at a turnout that was still under 60 percent of so-called "eligibles." But never mind.

The point is, when the Court tried to pump it up, why did the voting rate fall? I say again, a big reason is that the unions collapsed and the farmer granges disappeared. There were no unions in the cities or granges in the rural areas to get working people to the polls. Yet there is a second reason why many who were in the majority began to drop out.

The Constitution "morphed." From 1938 to 1975 the Court went all out to push "majority" rule; but by the end of this period, we were well on the way to the very opposite—not majority but minority rule. That's the paradox. How, if everyone was pushing majority rule, could we end up with more minority rule?

To explain how this could happen, here's the story of the "Fourth Republic."

Chapter Nine
The Rise and Fall of the "Fourth Republic"

Some years ago, a Yale Law professor, Bruce Ackerman, argued in a book, *We the People: Foundations* (1991), that America has had three separate "foundings," or really three different types of republics. The first was in 1787. The second was after the Civil War. The third was during the New Deal of the 1930s. Although the New Deal did not change the Constitution formally, we have had three distinctive types of "republics." But since then we've had a fourth republic. This Fourth Republic began in the 1970s and it's the one under which you and I have lived.

Maybe a fifth republic is about to begin, after the 2004 election.

But it's under the Fourth Republic that the rule of law collapsed. Maybe you were not aware that we started a fourth republic. It was never in the news as such. It grew bit by bit out of the deadlock between the political parties. I mean the divided government that began in 1968 with the election of Nixon and a Democratic Congress, and may have ended at last in 2004 with the re-election of George W. Bush.

From 1968 to 2004, for the longest time ever in American history, neither party was in control. This was as novel as a New Deal.

It's true.

Basically, if we ever went from contract to tort, it was in our Constitution at this time. From check-and-balance we went to punch-and-smash-mouth. Legislative and Executive tried to one-up the other, and each branch became less accountable to the people. In the end, the Court itself became less accountable, too.

First, the Senate became less accountable: it now takes not 50 but 60 votes to do anything important. Second, the House became less accountable: it is now so gerrymandered that almost no one can be removed. Third, the President became less accountable. Thanks to the Electoral College, the candidates now focus on a few battleground states, in a much more self-conscious way than before. For this one national office, we really vote now in about ten states instead of fifty. Fourth, though we still talk of an Imperial President, we have made the executive much weaker. We impeach him. Prosecute him. At least if he is not of the right party. As a result, a less accountable Congress is now stronger than he. And finally, the Court is less accountable. It no longer engages in judicial review to help along majority rule. Look at *Bush v. Gore*. Now the rule is, if people are being cheated of the right to vote, that's precisely the time the Court should not intervene.

Every branch of our government is less accountable to the majority. And the President, the one real tribune of the people, has lost most of his power. Does this seem far fetched? Fine. Let's start over.

1. The Senate

It is one hell of a thing that it now takes three fifths of the Senate to pass virtually any important bill. From 1787 until I got out of law school, it only took a simple majority. In 1975, we "reformed" the old filibuster rule, which took two thirds. Yes, there was always a filibuster, but it was used only on very rare occasions, when some liberal tried to stop black people from being lynched. Very, very rare. But after the civil rights revolution, the South came to the North and said in a very charming Southern accent:

"Oh Northerners, let's not get rid of the filibuster."

"No?"

"No, let's change it from 67 to 60 votes. We promise never again will we use it to hurt black people. Never. Never again."

Like there was a rainbow in the sky. So the North agreed. Fine. And once it was changed from 67 to 60 votes, from two thirds to three fifths, the South and the GOP began to use it nearly every time for every major bill. At least they began to do so by the Clinton era.

If there is a single proof of the collapse of the rule of law in America, it's the fact that no one knows how many votes it takes to pass a bill in Congress. Literally. If America ever applied for a loan at the World Bank and had to fill out an application and the application asked, how-many-votes-does-it-take-to-pass-a-bill?, we would have to answer, "We really don't know." Imagine if a country like Sri Lanka tried saying that.

The Senate's always been awful, throughout our history. That's why there is no labor law reform. The Senate blocked it. No national health care. The Senate blocked it. No social democracy. The Senate blocked it. "But that was in the past," you say. OK, but that's why today the "majority" of those who still vote are as skewed to the right as they are. Because in the 1930s and '40s, even the 1990s, the real majority could not get what they wanted. That's why Carter and Clinton could not accomplish much even though the Democrats had the Congress.

The reason the Senate's so bad is that every state has two votes. But come on, the political scientists say, "Do small states have any different interest from the large states?" They think that is what we anti-Senate people hate. It isn't. Our answer is, "Wake up! The war in American history has not been between smaller and larger states. It's a war between or among the various regions. The South as a region has long had an unfair veto in the Senate. From 1930 to 1975, they could stop America from having a real European-type social democracy, even though they were a minority region. Today, the Red States have an unfair advantage too. Thanks to the wacky way the 50 states carve up the total national yardage, the Reds get a way unfair lead over the Blues. The Reds can govern in the Senate—as the poor Blues can never hope to do."

Result: the right looks like it can govern, especially in times of crisis. The left never looks that way.

But doesn't a filibuster let us deliberate? Sure, I can see an argument in its favor, if—and I say IF—a pre-filibuster Senate were already fair, i.e., one-person, one-vote, like the states have to be because of *Baker v. Carr*. But the Senate was already skewed.

By what logic, when we started a Fourth Republic, did we go from a pattern of usually 50 to usually 60 votes so as to skew it even more? Nothing could be less democratic. Except of course what happened to the House!

2. The House

The House is now out of popular control. This is supposed to be the chamber that the people elect. But thanks to the new gerrymandering-by-computer and the ease of processing data on party registration, state legislatures now determine who will hold the US House seats.

But how can this be constitutional? For gerry-mandering is nothing but a "law." It is a law that separates people from each other because of how they express themselves politically. "You, Ms. A, go over to this District." "You, Mr. B., move over this way, to this district." In other words, it is a colossal violation of our First Amendment rights. It is hard to imagine the likes of it. Suppose my state, Illinois, passed a law that only 40 percent of the people in Lake County or whatever could be registered Democrats. One day, I'm at home. The sheriff knocks at the door: "I'm sorry, you'll have to move to Cook County. We have information that you're a Democrat, and we're already over 40 percent here."

Now I realize gerrymandering works in a more velvet way. But it comes down to the same thing: People have to up and move from one Congressional district to another because of how they have expressed their views. So far as I can tell, in no other country on the planet, even the old South Africa, does such a relocation of the population—on paper anyway—go on. They put us into boxes. Not boxcars. But we are moved around just the same. And the purpose is to make sure that no one in Congress is accountable. Could there be anything worse? Yes.

3. The Presidency

Forget the Senate. The House. The worst is the Presidency.

We now get to vote for President in only about ten of our fifty states. Only in "battleground" states. That's the real signature of the Fourth Republic. In the other states—California, New York—the rest of us just vote for the fun of it.

But isn't it true that we have always had an Electoral College?

True, yet in the America of our parents, they didn't hear it on TV over and over. Or they forgot. Or they engaged in a willing suspension of disbelief. Now we know. So people stop attending church. They drop out of any civic life at all.

Because why vote? The House is safe. Four fifths of the Electoral College is decided. A few Senate seats are up for grabs, but the Senate exists only to frustrate the majority. All this means I will vote only if I understand I can help to put in place a gridlock. Still we write editorials urging people to vote. "Remember the Founders, etc." Of course some of the Founders wanted only land owners to vote. They did not imagine the poor or the landless or women voting too. That's why our Constitution has no majority rule. Still, to be fair to the Founders, our own Fourth Republic is probably less democratic than even they wanted. I think the lack of accountability in the House would shock them.

The more that voters dropped out, the more gridlock we had. And the more gridlock we had, the more voters dropped out. After thirty years of gridlock, and the new barriers to majority rule, I think we should be thankful so many still vote. Or at least, they do for President.

Now that's curious because the President himself is so much weaker. It seems clear that

Congress has the upper hand. Now that it is relatively
free of popular control, Congress is relatively free to
destroy a sitting President. Maybe this was not true at
the start, though the Democrats in Congress did drive
Nixon from office. But the longer that one party had
the Congress and the other had the Presidency, the
weaker on the whole the Presidency became. By the
end of the century, even a Paula Jones could sue a
President and drive him from office. Imagine that a
President was impeached for lying about a side issue
in a deposition in a civil case that a federal judge
dismissed for failure to state a claim!

I still can't really imagine it.

This war between Congress and the President
has also undermined the rule of law because we fought
it out, at the national level, by lawless and extra-legal
means. In a constitutional sense, we had to improvise
as we went along. Consider the lawless or extra-legal
way it went:

- The use of a Special Prosecutor as a perennial
  Grand Inquisitor
- The use of Impeachment for matters that
  were not criminal
- The law breaking by the President to get around
  Congress—in the Iran-Contra case and others
- The way the Supreme Court stepped in to break
  the 2000 deadlock

In *Bush v. Gore*, the Supreme Court stepped in
because as Justice Kennedy supposedly said,
"Somebody had to decide it." If the Court did not put

in Bush, Congress would have put him in. In *Bush v. Gore*, the Court did not just step in to decide a particular election, however important; it stepped in to end the gridlock, the Thirty Years' War, this period of extra-legal conflict. In that sense, the real winner of *Bush v. Gore* was Congress.

At last the gridlock was over. The Congress had the President it wanted.

Some are astonished that Bush went on to do so much with such a "narrow" mandate. They miss what really happened. For with Bush's election, the Congress at last was entirely in control. It had to deal with a temporary defection in the Senate. But after the Congressional election in 2002, everything was in place for a new kind of republic, a fifth republic, with one Gaullist-type party in charge.

If Kerry had been elected, we would have gone back to the disorder of the old Fourth Republic. Given that the Congress is Republican for good and given the need now to have a strong Executive, it is hard to see how a Democrat in the White House is really plausible—at least for the near future. I kept waiting in the debates for someone to ask poor Kerry the obvious, "Mr. Kerry, won't you be a crippled President from the day of your swearing in, with a Republican Congress out to harass and perhaps impeach you?"

In a small but ominous way, the Swift Boat ads brought home what would happen if the voters elected Kerry. Most people grasped that the Swift Boat ads were lies. Yet it actually helped Bush for people to see that the ads were simply lies. See? Kerry can't protect himself even from these lies. Remember what we did to Clinton. Just wait and see what we will do to him. Of course as a Democrat who saw Bush and Kerry in their mismatched debates, I have far more trust in Kerry. He is much the stronger man. Still, I cringe at what would have happened had Kerry been elected.

The President now is no match for the Congress. Thanks to the deficit and deregulation, the President has—well, he has lost his staff. The best and brightest do not go into his service. He does not have enough of a civil service, or enough of a high caliber one, to execute the laws or to do so effectively. He does not have enough food inspectors, health inspectors or rail inspectors. He does not have enough people to guard the borders or to watch the ports.

In *The End of Liberalism* (1969), a famous book of my youth, Theodore Lowi argued that in making laws, Congress gave the Executive too much discretion, too much power. He predicted this would undermine the rule of law.

Now in my middle age, I think it's just the opposite. Congress has tried to shrink the Executive. The threat is to limit the ability of the Executive to carry out the law.

4. The Supreme Court

At the end of this Fourth Republic, at least the gridlock is over. At least we are spared now the spectacle of our elected leaders acting extra-legally and engaging in various kinds of constitutional torts.

But the way the Supreme Court ended the gridlock not only discredited the rule of law even more but the Court itself as an institution. It was not so bad that the Court decided the case. Someone had to. Nor that it ruled in Bush's favour. Someone had to win.

What was so bad was that the Court temporarily stayed the counting of the vote. Even worse than the stay was Justice Scalia's reason: that it would cause "irreparable harm" if the citizens of our democracy knew how the vote came out. It would be irreparably harmful if We the People were to know how We the People had really voted!

Doesn't that deserve an exclamation point? If *Bush v. Gore* gave birth to a new, or fifth, republic, the stay of the voting will be its mark of Cain.

In the first big case of the new century, it was clear we had come a long, long way from footnote 4 of *Carolene Products*. No longer was the rationale to clear the channels of political change or facilitate majority rule. To facilitate majority rule might now well constitute irreparable harm.

Why should the Court push majority rule in a country in which the majority did not vote? Now some may quibble about the word "majority." But it was certainly not a majority in Florida if we count the half a million voters excluded because once in their lives they had served time in a prison. If those half a million voters in Florida had been allowed to vote, Bush would have lost the state of Florida twice, not just in 2000 but in 2004.

And then there are all the other exclusions, more subtle, as the federal courts abandon footnote 4 of *Carolene Products* and look the other way.

Let me testify to this indifference from my personal experience. I just brought a voting rights case and lost. Here was the issue: Unlike most states, in Illinois there is no right to vote absentee or by mail automatically. Nor is there any possibility for "early" voting as in Texas or Florida. In Illinois, a voter has to vote, in person, at the polls—unless he or she "expects" to be "out of the county" under the state's archaic absentee ballot law. No election board checks up on people, and no state agency has ever attempted to enforce the law. Nor until I filed a suit had anyone ever tried to interpret the law either. For example, what does the term "out of the county" mean, as millions every day drive along the interstates? Indeed what does the term "expect" mean? No one knows. In real life the political machines exploit the ambiguity of the law to get their people the absentee ballots and turn out their own respective votes.

So I brought a suit to challenge this law which no one has interpreted or enforced and which has invited massive fraud. I represented five working mothers, who have to juggle commutes, full-time jobs, child care, and just wanted to vote, without having to lie: "I 'expect' to be 'out of the county.'"

Of course I lost. I lost even at the pleading stage. It didn't matter how much vote fraud we alleged, the court just threw us out. The panel said that if a state wants to curb voting "opportunities," a court should just defer. Defer! It is the very opposite of what a court is supposed to do under *Carolene Products*. Why defer? Because the right to vote, the Court of Appeals said, is simply not that important.

That's right: the right to vote is not important. This ruling disturbs me for two reasons. First, there's my vanity as a lawyer. After the oral argument, I really thought we'd won. Second, these judges may be conservatives but they were rationalists. They were not "Federalists." They were not impressed with Bork. It made me realize that even when people are on the same side with respect to the Enlightenment, we still have the old differences between Jefferson and Hamilton.

What do the Hamiltonians want? Economic efficiency. And what do we Jeffersonians want? Popular sovereignty. We want the poor to have a bigger stake in things. But at this moment as more and more people drop out and we have less control over them as a result, we think that maybe the Hamiltonians should want this too. If their Enlightenment ever begins to burn and crackle, they may be sorry they did not think in bigger terms.

If the right to vote is not important and footnote 4 is in demise, I am not sure how we can go about restoring the rule of law. Where else can we look?

Chapter Ten
In A Distant Country

Maybe we can look abroad.

Since *Bush v. Gore*, two very strange things have happened. First, in Bush's first term and contrary to prediction, nobody on the Court resigned. Some Justices may have thought, "I can't go in his first term, since I'm the one who put him in." Second, even more contrary to prediction, the Court has begun citing international law. It did so in *Jenkins v. Texas*, which struck down a Texas law that made a crime of sodomy. Justice Kennedy, who seems to feel the most guilt over *Bush v. Gore*, wrote the opinion. He cited the law in other countries.

It was a Republican appointee who broke the taboo.

Then came the Guantánamo case. The majority cited international law again. It seems we lawyers can now invoke it—sometimes. If and when Bush II appointees get on the Court, this little springtime in the law could be over very fast. But why did a Bush I conservative like Kennedy let us even argue it? It may be the only way to check and balance Bush II and the new right in the Congress.

Remember, our Fourth Republic, the era of constitutional civil war, is over. Legally we are in a new world. With Congress not as likely now to check the Executive or vice versa, the Court may need a new source of authority to keep both of them from running wild. There are other good reasons to cite the law of other nations.

It is probably what the Founders—Madison, Hamilton, et al.—would do: take the "best practices" of other countries. To take "best practices" was an Enlightenment type of thing. You and I wouldn't understand it. But back in the Age of Reason, that's how they wrote not only the Constitution but some of our first laws. The Alien Tort Claims Act, for example. It literally says that the courts can apply "the law of nations."

Yet here's an even better reason to cite the law of other nations.

This type of law gives us an external standard, outside of ourselves; it lets us know what we in turn would do if we had the majority rule or one-person, one-vote that these other countries do. The logic is

Cartesian. Take a set of well-off constitutional democracies: one, two, three, four… ten. Unlike the US, all of them have one-person, one-vote. If all ten adopt Legal Principle A, then it seems that under the same majority rule we would do the same. "But, wait," some will say, "you're leaving out our culture!" But I factor out the culture. It is tainted by the fact that we do not have majority rule based on one-person, one-vote. That's why I pick ten which have it: France, Japan, Canada, Australia, etc. Let's say all ten come out with A. Therefore, I conclude that if we had one-person, one-vote, as in countries one through ten, we'd come out with—A.

Of course I'm picking rich democracies, with no mass poverty. We do have mass poverty. It may be better to compare what we do with what they do in China. Still, I'd hate to set the bar so low as to compare us with Russia or the Congo.

Some of the new right would. "If you don't like it here, go to Russia or the Congo."

Yet in the end I doubt we can smuggle in the legal norms of other nations. This kind of approach runs up against a problem. Maybe the norms of the ten nations would be ours if we had the same majority rule. But we do not have the same majority rule. Whether or not they would be our norms, we did not vote them in.

If I try to put them in as a lawyer, I am putting in a rule of law to which no one gives consent, in fact. I am like a young officer in the British Empire, out to bring the rule of law to India. It may be a fine rule of law, but it is not one to which India gives consent.

One day, sooner or later, the people of India will sit there, massively disobedient, and simply toss us out.

When I look at the international law or treaty law that does exist here, that treaty law is the law that is in the biggest shambles. Let's take the right of a foreign person, who is arrested here, to get in touch with that person's consulate. This is the right set out in Article 36 of the Vienna Convention on Consular Relations. This is a treaty the US ratified, incredibly enough. But is the treaty in effect? Yes and no. It depends.

Whether the treaty is in effect depends on where in America you're arrested.

In Chicago, sure you have the right. Want to phone your consul? The cops are quick to ask you. But that's because in this town, the Latinos are so powerful politically. On the other hand, if you're arrested out in Cicero, no one's going to tell you. In Cicero, you don't have the right at all. Why? The Latinos don't have the clout politically to get Cicero to tell you.

Meanwhile, the State Department takes no responsibility. "You have to take it up with the states." In some states, foreign nationals are arrested, denied all rights, and end up on Death Row. In other states— hey, the treaty's in effect!

That's why the World Court has asked that the US review the death sentences of (mostly) Mexicans who had the bad luck to be picked up in states where there is "no Article 36." These are people picked up in places where the Latinos do not have the clout politically to put the law in effect.

To its credit, the Supreme Court has decided to hear the case and consider the disparities. What will it do? Hard to say. But it seems we could treat the disparity in enforcement of this treaty right as a problem not of international law but of American civil rights law. It really is a problem of race. If Latinos have enough power, there's enforcement. If they lack the power, there is none. We could take it up in the traditional categories of Fourteenth Amendment race law.

But that's the sorry tale of a right under a treaty we ratified. What hope is there for rights to which we did not formally consent or ratify? Think of all the other legal norms that are not so clearly entangled with the local racial politics of a Chicago or Cicero. I mean just plain old garden-variety prohibitions against barbarity and torture.

I despair we can really apply such prohibitions here, by judicial fiat. The fiat runs up against the enormity of the Third Big Fact I wrote about: our gulag-growth of prisons.

Prison may be just too big a thing for our courts now to control. We don't go there; we can't bear it; we don't even want to know. As inequality increases, the prisons will get bigger. Perhaps not next year, but over the next ten years—and the next twenty, and the next half century.

And as prisons get even bigger, it will become harder to put in human rights law. The prosecutors are too strong. The police are too strong. The prison guards are too strong. The new right is already too strong, for us to dream that we can usher in some golden age of human rights.

Consider these two stories.

First Story: In the past year or so, the Supreme Court has been unable to get the Fifth Circuit even to pretend to apply its instructions in death penalty cases in Texas and Louisiana. So reports the *New York Times* on the front page of the Sunday, November 14, 2004 edition. The Fifth Circuit is not covertly but openly defying the Court in specific death penalty cases. After one remand, the Fifth Circuit quoted and followed Clarence Thomas' sole dissent, and not the majority opinion—in the very case before it.

It's one thing for a Court of Appeals to evade a controlling legal authority. But it's quite another thing to defy a specific instruction from the Supreme Court itself, indeed, to mock and taunt the Court as well. And if judges of the Fifth Circuit can act like this, try to imagine what our cops and our prison guards might do.

Second Story: The rage everywhere against the International Criminal Court (ICC). By resolution of December 2001, Congress declared a war upon The Hague. The resolution says that if any US soldier is put on trial before the ICC, the President can attack. Imagine: even before 9/11, we had started debating a resolution to use shock and awe on Holland.

Moreover, it passed.

Back then I could not conceive US soldiers committing the kind of crimes that would lead to such a trial. I'm afraid I can conceive it now. The Congressional resolution is still ridiculous, of course. If America were part of the ICC, America and Europe would run it, more or less the way they run the UN and every other global entity. Is it childish, then, to declare war on Holland? No, it's worse than childish. And if the leaders of the Congress can act like this, try to imagine what our cops and our prison guards might do.

*****

Normally I would want to end my essay here, in despair. But since this is a pamphlet, it is expected that I end it with a call to arms. I should propose some kind of approach to bring back the rule of law.

So my friends tell me. People like to see "A Plan." Ah, but it's often so contrived! It's only a writer who thinks there can be one "A Plan." In real life there can never really be "A Plan"—except to show up at work and keep on answering your phone.

That being said, I guess I have "A Plan." There are two parts to this Plan. First, we should try to bring back contract and trust law at the state level. The aim is to have the rule of law in a state or two, as it were in miniature. Second—and again—we should try to argue for more majority rule through the courts. We have to argue again for *Carolene Products* footnote 4. "But we tried footnote 4!" Then we have to try the thing again—only this time on a vastly bigger scale.

But let's turn first to the states, or the few states where we have a chance to enact some good laws. Forget Congress and the White House for now. Let's govern from the Blue States; at least they have one-person, one-vote. But what can we do? Here's an example from employment law. In Chapter Two I complained about how we have gone from Contract to Tort. But a state would be free to pass a law that says, "No one can be fired except for just cause." In a formalistic sense, OK, it's still a "tort" and not a "contract." We stop peering into people's hearts and look at their external conduct.

Result? The law is more rational. We can begin to develop something like a Rule of Reason in the way we encounter the law.

Or let's take the law of trusts, which has collapsed. As I argued above, our charitable institutions have gone into a kind of racketeering. There is a way to fix it, however, by changing who gets on the board. Once I would have said, "Put real Methodists on the boards of Methodist hospitals. Or make sure that half of these boards have directors with real backgrounds in charity and religious work. Prohibit any one who has any business ties with the not-for-profit."

But one of my friends in labor scoffs, "You mean put on more nuns? They're the worst of the union busters." She's right. The real answer is not to change the directors, but the people to whom they are accountable. No one on the board is accountable to any group outside the board. There are no real "settlors." (They're dead, or never existed.) There are no stockholders. There are no stakeholders. At least a corporate board is accountable to shareholders. So what to do? I say, if the not-for-profit has over 50 employees, let them elect a third of the directors. At least these directors would owe their seats to somebody other than a fellow director. There would be some outside voice. Admittedly, that's a fix one would expect from a labor lawyer like me. But in the case of a hospital, who would have a better sense of the charity's mission than a nurse who chose to do charity work? And if she were on a board, she would truly be independent because she is elected by someone other than the director sitting next to her.

In administrative law there is also a fix, but it is a lot more ambitious. It is to break up the office of the state attorney general. Or create a new position, a Public Guardian, whose mission is not to defend the state but to sue it. Look at Elliot Spitzer: he can sue an Aetna but not the state department of insurance. Which of the two is worse? But Spitzer has a conflict of interest. He is supposed to defend the state department of insurance. The way to police the state is to free up the attorney general so that the office has no conflict of interest. Create an AG who has no role in representing or defending any public agency. In a time of the de-funding of law enforcement, it is a way to have some check and balance. Set one part of the state against the other. Let two ambitious elected lawyers fight it out. In a time of de-regulation, it is a way to cut down on the erratic use of vigilantes and keep up the pressure on the Executive to execute the laws.

Of course, we need other changes too.

But we may not get them. Even if we did, these "changes" and others may all be for nought unless we get back a bit more "majority rule." We need a new republic, or we need to jump start the old one. How? Well, remember, I'm only a lawyer. So all I can think of is to bring litigation. I'm sorry, I'm sorry! Maybe it's better to give up. Maybe it only would amount to a *cri de coeur* in the courts.

Yet with a few lawsuits and one or two legislative fixes, here's how we might do it.

First: Sue on gerrymandering.

Peter Levine at the University of Maryland tells me, "If you ask political scientists what is the biggest threat to the republic, most of them will say, 'It's the gerrymandering of Congress.'" Why does the Court not get rid of it? Well, the plaintiffs do not want to get rid of it, not entirely. Instead they argue, "Oh, some gerrymandering is OK, but in this case, it's too much." So judges like Scalia say, "Well, what is 'too much'?" He can then scoff, "Cases like these are not even justiciable." And as the parties argue them, he is probably right. The problem is that the cases are controlled by two parties each of whom wants to save "reasonable" gerrymandering for itself.

Besides, no court wants to look at map after map. "Your Honor, they should not run the line down Maple Street, but over here down Elm Street."

The solution: Sue on the First Amendment to get rid of all. Tell the Court, "We don't want you to keep looking at all these maps. We want you to require the state to change the process by which the maps are made." If it is unlawful to use our speech or political expression to divide us up into different districts, the court ought to prohibit any use of these criteria in the process of drawing up a congressional map. The court should stop poring over the damn maps and just order the state to come up with a neutral process. "But you can't remove politics from

this process," says my friend R. Sure you can. Iowa
has done it. It is not all that hard. In the case of Iowa,
there is a commission with two Democrats and two
Republicans; the four then elect a neutral member to
break a tie. They then appoint a staff. The staff is not
allowed to look at voter registration records or electoral outcomes. They produce three maps. The Iowa
legislature can only vote them up or down.

The Iowa model may not fit a bigger state.
Fine. Let each state come up with its own process,
provided it has at least the same guarantee of neutral-
ity. If the court can sign off on the process, state by
state, it never has to look at another congressional
map.

Second: Deal on the filibuster.

But here, alas, no court will ever toss out the
filibuster. Or the 60-vote rule. Rule 22.

It is partly because no one has "standing;" no
court will allow you and me to bring a suit to knock
out an internal Senate rule.

So?

Well, at the moment, the Republicans want to
deal on the filibuster. Not end it, but mend it. End it
only for judicial nominations, so that even the nutti-
est Federalist Society member can get on the
Supreme Court. After all, Bush may get up to four
Supreme Court nominations. Being a liberal I'd like
to check him by filibuster. But I think the Democrats
should give it up. Give it all up, the whole filibuster,
forever.

Some of my friends on the left will say:
WHAT? ARE YOU CRAZY?

Wait! I didn't say NOW. We should give it up after 2008, in the next President's term. It is only fair to the voters to know that next time they elect a Republican, we will be playing under different rules.

And don't give it up for free. At least get something for it. Like a deal that gerrymandering of the House becomes illegal too—if we cannot otherwise win our case in the courts.

Third: Use game theory to get out of the Electoral College.

Abolish the Electoral College by amending the Constitution? Too many little states could block it. Yet Maine offers a clue as to how we might end it without a formal amendment to the Constitution. By state law, Maine sends a "split" group of delegates who divide their votes for Bush and Kerry in the ratio of the popular vote in that state. Other states hesitate. Why would the majority in a pro-Bush or pro-Kerry state want to give up the respective Bush or Kerry "lock"? The result is that no state follows Maine. But here's an idea: A state could enact a Maine-type law, but hold it from taking effect until states with 75 percent of the population also put in effect the same law. In theory, that could be as few as 20 or 25 states.

Still, what of the hold outs? First, they'd be freak cases. They'd be under huge pressure to take the same line. Second, if they do try to hang on, sue them in the state courts. They'd be depriving their citizens of the same right to vote as the vast majority of Americans.

Fourth: Get rid of voter registration.

Why? Because some states are already moving to register all eligible citizens for jury duty. The reason, of course, is that we do not have enough registered voters to fill out our juries. I bemoaned all of this in chapter four. But if a state has to list all its eligible citizens, then it can toss away its list of registered voters. The only reason to make people register to vote is to make sure they're citizens. But a jury commissioner will now have a list of all citizens! Or should. So why don't the election boards use the same list?

In Illinois, a jury commissioner gets a "tape" of state photo IDs, like driver's licenses, etc. Then the commissioner has to "canvass" to see who is a citizen. Yes, some counties really do end up listing every eligible citizen. I checked, or my friend Tony did. If some do it, they all could. And if they all do it, then the US becomes like Australia or Canada. There, it is the state that registers the voter rather than the other way around. But what if the states don't register everyone for jury duty? Sue them. After all, jury duty is a burden that should be equally imposed.

Once the state has made this big list, there'd be no point in using the old voter registration rolls. And no legal reason for it. To prevent fraud? The big list, based on photo IDs, would be better than the old smaller one at preventing fraud.

In short, either the state drops the old imperfect list for the new list and lets everyone vote, or some civic-minded plaintiff should take the state to court. So let's assume the state has a duty now to register everyone, if only because it has to do it to fill out the juries. Then what's next?

Fifth: Mail the ballot to everyone.

Mail a ballot automatically to every registered voter. Oregon does it now. Here the idea is more ambitious. First, register everyone. Then, mail a ballot to everyone: Yes, every US citizen. One day, we will have to do it anyway. We will do it for the same reason Oregon did it. Like many states, Oregon allowed voters to request "absentee" ballots by mail whether they were absent from the state or not. (Seventeen states now do so.) Millions began to vote by mail. Soon Oregon had two different election processes: a mail ballot used generally by the more-educated, higher income voters; and an in-person polling ballot, used more by less-educated, lower income voters who did not go to the trouble of applying for an absentee ballot. Oregon gave up this complex system and went to one all-mail ballot. Any other way was too much trouble.

But then, how can any way other than Oregon's be legal? In many states, we now have one voting system used more by higher income people and another one used more by lower income people. Everyone ought to be on the same level. Moreover, given the long, long ballot that Americans have to fill out, it is hard to vote intelligently except by mail. Imagine standing in a polling place and marking a ballot with 40 or more races—as we do in Illinois! Finally, an all-mail ballot leaves the perfect paper trail.

Sixth: Sue to get civics.

In the long run, we have to teach kids that they have a moral obligation to vote, a duty. We have to teach it over and over. The problem is, few schools teach civics in the old schoolhouse sense. Some teach "government," but not civics, not the way it used to be taught. A few schools do teach "problems of democracy" or "current affairs." Or they teach some form of civics with extra bells and whistles. But if even one public school is teaching kids how to vote more effectively, then every kid in every school is entitled to the same. For "civics" is a form of state assistance in the exercise of our right to vote. Under *Bush v. Gore* and the equal protection clause of the Fourteenth Amendment, whatever the state is doing for some of our children they should do for all of them, every single one.

How nice if every state just passed a law requiring, and funding, four years of civics in every public school. Some might. Others won't. In the states we fail to pass such laws, we ought to cite *Bush v. Gore* and take them into court.

Would all the fixes in The Plan really work? I do not know. Perhaps there are better plans. But if we could inch America a bit more to majority rule, we'd have a different set of laws. We'd have laws more like those of countries in Europe and in Australia and Canada. Then our laws would make us feel safer—or simply less fearful. Or less in fear of the kind of random injury, like loss of job, loss of pension, even loss of law and order, which makes us now resort to tort.

The law as well would be more secure. For it would have a truer, purer kind of consent. I like to think that one day, the Bishop of Rockford, and the rest of us, will have the rule of law we want. While that America may seem to me like a distant country, it may be closer than I think.

Conclusion

If all that happened, then we would be on the same path that other countries are. It is often said, on the right, that we Americans are going one way, while the Europeans are going another. But sometimes I think it is not just in Europe but all the other democracies that people are going a different way: toward more human rights, toward more international law. It would be awful to think that Americans are going one way, and human beings are going another. No, that's not true. Yet, something is wrong. And these peoples in the other developed countries of the world are a mirror image of what we in America would think and do, if we had a similar type of rule of law under a similar type of constitution.

But we don't.

And the current war on terror is a big departure from any other war in our history, for two reasons. First, our war leaders—Lincoln, Wilson, Roosevelt—always put the rationale for war in terms of law. Lincoln the lawyer did so. Wilson had the Fourteen Points. FDR looked forward to a genuine international law, like the UN Charter. Bush never mentions "law" at all. If one did a LEXIS search of his speeches, I doubt the word "law" would ever appear, except incidentally, the way it might appear if hundreds of monkeys were pounding typewriters to turn out presidential speeches.

Instead, there is one word: "liberty." Over and over. Not "law." Not "justice." The way he uses "liberty" so obsessively over and over seems to be his way of telling us to be fearful, that nothing is predictable or determined.

The Europeans are different. They talk much more about "the law." That's why the new right disdains them so. These people in other countries—they're all so "moral" and "legalistic." I hate to end by invoking Kant, but I can't resist. The neo-cons are always attacking Kant. And Kantian morality. Let's give the man a chance to answer them all back. Kant would say, I think, if he were around: "The Europeans are not better than the Americans. They are not more virtuous. They are not better people. Americans are not going one way while human beings at least in the wealthy democracies seem to be going another." No, but the Europeans do use the word "law." They talk about the "the law." They put things in terms of "the rule of law." Just by using the word "law" or the phrase "rule of law" the Europeans act better and more morally. It's literally saying the word "law" and arguing about the "law" that makes them act better than in their heart of hearts they really are.

That's my excuse for the title of this essay and for talking about our problems as Americans as problems with the rule of law. Maybe there is nothing else I can accomplish, for my country or for myself, but to repeat over and over: the law.

The law, the law, the law, the law—more and more, we must think about and talk about and argue about the law. If we do so, we may act better than the people that we really are. ■

Also available from Prickly Paradigm Press: